Trouble Blows West

A GINNIE WEST ADVENTURE

Book Two

Elizabeth Johnson,

May all of

your

Troubles

Blow West!

Monique

Bucheger

MONIQUE BUCHEGER

Trouble Blows West: A Ginnie West Adventure

Text Copyright © 2013 Monique Bucheger.
Illustration Copyright © 2013 Mikey Brooks.
Cover design by Lost Treasure Illustrating.
Published by True West Publishing.

Printed in the United States of America

Charleston, South Carolina

ISBN-13:978-1939993106
ISBN-10:1939993105

DEDICATION

This book is dedicated to the people who helped me weave my story. It would not have been the same without you.

Mrs. Johnson: It's taken me too long to write the books that you knew I would, but thank you for being my very first cheerleader. This is for you. ☺ I pray each of my children have many teachers like you in their lives.

Fast Forward 20 years: Lola, Trudy, and Beth: Thank you for supporting me by reading my first, not-so-well written drafts and falling in love with the West family anyway. ☺

Scoot, Pauline, Scott, N.B., Suzanne, Lance, Sheila and Debbie and Stephanie… the Wests and I thank you for your diligence in helping me strengthen their story and present them in the most entertaining, heartwarming ways.

To Mikey Brooks: I love what you do for the Wests'. ☺

Anniqa, Daniel, Cassie, Ryan, Kristen, Andrew, Aeron, Brioni, Adam, Luisa, Ian, Aedric… May each of your dreams come true and may you each have many dreams to dream.

And to my husband, Kurt… your support has been sustaining and incredible and I love you even more than I did twenty-seven years ago when we started our married journey together.

CONTENTS

WEST FAMILY TREE

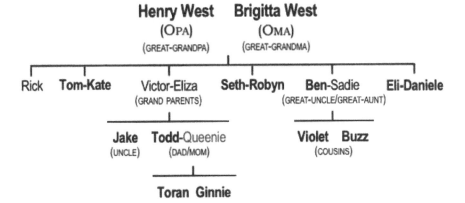

Henry West
(OPA)
(GREAT-GRANDPA)

Brigitta West
(OMA)
(GREAT-GRANDMA)

Rick   **Tom**-Kate   Victor-Eliza   **Seth-Robyn**   **Ben**-Sadie   Eli-**Daniele**
(GRAND PARENTS)   (GREAT-UNCLE/GREAT-AUNT)

Jake   Todd-Queenie   **Violet   Buzz**
(UNCLE)   (DAD/MOM)   (COUSINS)

Toran   Ginnie

Bold denotes living family members

CHAPTER ONE:
THE FIGHT

A hush fell over the school cafeteria.

Ginnie West looked up just in time to see trouble brewing in the form of the biggest bully in sixth grade.

Pierce Owens stomped his way toward her twin brother, his face twisted with fury. "Toran West, you're toast!"

Swallowing hard, Ginnie knew this day would not end well. She jumped to her feet, her blonde braids thumping her back. "Go away, Pierce!"

Toran pushed his chair away from the rectangular table. "Ginnie, let me handle this."

"No way!" Ginnie's whole body tensed as she glared at Pierce. "Toran isn't going to fight with you."

Heads swiveled left and right.

Pierce glowered angrily, his eyes forming slits. "I was right. And you're going to pay, West!"

Toran stood, shaking his head like an Etch-A-Sketch. "What are you talking about?"

Her twin's stick-thin frame next to Pierce's taller and rounder body reminded Ginnie of the number ten, with the '0' being overly round and out of proportion to the '1'.

The thought made her giggle.

Pierce shot her a warning glare and then poked his finger in Toran's chest.

"Hey! Keep your hands to yourself!" Ginnie demanded.

Pierce poked Toran again.

Toran backed up.

Pierce leaned forward. "You cheated and made me look stupid! Pierce Owens doesn't let nobody make him look stupid."

"Too late. Nobody has to *help* you look stupid!" Ginnie said, going around the table to join her brother, heart pounding. "You're so stupid you think a quarterback is a refund."

Toran's eyes widened. Half of their friends laughed. The other half dropped their jaws in stunned horror.

Concern wormed its way into Ginnie's belly as she realized too late that taking on Pierce wasn't the smartest thing she'd ever done.

Austin Chandler scrambled to Toran's other side. "Move back, Pierce!"

Oh, good. Austin has my back. We've got this. The Three Musketeers ride again. Ginnie smiled at Austin with more confidence than she felt and then turned back to Pierce. "You heard him, move it."

Pierce ignored Austin, then scowled at Ginnie. "You're not part of this!"

"I am *now*." Ginnie put herself squarely between Toran and harm's way. "You mess with my brother … you mess with me." Pierce towered over her, but that didn't matter. No one was flattening Toran under her watch.

"Stop!" Toran demanded, grabbing her arm. "I've got this."

She shrugged off her brother's hand. "Not happening."

Pierce reached around Ginnie and yanked Toran's midnight blue polo shirtsleeve.

Ginnie didn't waste a second. She snatched at Pierce's hand, then sideswiped her foot behind his, shoving him with her forearm as hard as she could. He hit the floor with a thud.

A warm, happy feeling rushed over her as the room erupted in a mixture of thundering applause and mocking laughter.

Pierce blinked. Confusion colored his face. It was obvious he didn't expect that attack, and certainly not from a girl.

He scrambled to his feet, growing taller and more menacing.

Ginnie readied for the expected punch, hoping it wouldn't hurt too much. No way was she gonna let Pierce make her cry.

A teacher raced to their table, blowing her whistle. The shrill sound drowned out the growing voices.

Sugar beets!

Raising his fist, Pierce's face contorted into an angry tomato. "I'm gonna to take you down."

Her heartbeat tripled as Pierce neared.

Toran jumped in front of her, arms outstretched. "Your fight's with me."

When the bully charged forward, Ginnie elbowed Toran aside and raised her own fist.

"Her first," Pierce barked.

"You and what army?" Ginnie snapped. With Toran back in danger, Ginnie's mouth ran quicker than her brain. "The only things you take down are milkshakes and glazed doughnuts."

Giggles and guffaws burst out around the room.

Ginnie jerked back as Pierce lunged forward, barely missing his flying fists. *Yikes, he's big!*

The whistle screeched again. Pierce dropped his hands as Mrs. Ruby crooked her finger at Ginnie and then Pierce. "Come with me, you and you."

"I told you to stop," Toran muttered.

Why's he's so mad? I'm the one who just got busted. Ginnie shirked off her concern. Before she could address her brother, Austin offered a "thumb's up."

His deep blue eyes shone his admiration.

Ginnie beamed her pleasure.

Some kids behind Mrs. Ruby whistled, others called out: "Cool, Gin!" Still others scrambled to wipe smiles from their faces as Pierce seemed to count and memorize each one in turn.

"*Now,*"Mrs. Ruby ordered. "Both of you." She stood, waving her arms like a traffic officer, making a path through the crowd.

"Yes, ma'am." *At least I got to knock him on his can.* Ginnie grabbed her brownie and took a bite. *No sense wasting this.* From the corner of her eye she caught sight of her best friend, Tillie Taylor, chewing her lower lip and shaking her head.

"A-are you okay?" Tillie looked like a trapped doe in headlights.

Ginnie knew Tillie had been a worrywart since kindergarten. *Don't panic, Tillie. You've seen me in worse trouble than this.* Ginnie threw her a mischievous smile and wiggled her eyebrows.

When Tillie shook her head, returned the smile, and then rolled her eyes, Ginnie knew she had done her job and reassured her best friend. She turned back to Pierce.

His eyes bore through her. "This ain't the end of this," he hissed.

His chin wiggled as his face grew more purple, a bit like an eggplant, but not so attractive. His cheeks were as wide as his face was long, like an overblown balloon.

Ginnie whipped her head toward him, sending her blond braids flying. "For your sake, it better be, Pierce Owens, 'cuz there's only two ways this ends. I knock you on your can again or you beat up a girl. Neither way looks good—*for you.*"

Pierce had no time to retort.

Mrs. Ruby ushered them by the double doors.

A group of boys burst into the hall through the doors, pushing and chattering. One bumped into the pea-green lockers lining the hall. Outside, at recess, kids laughed and shouted.

"No talking. Just keep walking." Mrs. Ruby's lips drew a stern line as she herded them to the office and pointed at opposite walls. "Ginnie, sit here. Pierce, over there."

Four chairs lined each wall. Pierce dropped into a chair under the black wall clock, threatening, "Just wait until there aren't any teachers. You'll be sorry!"

Ginnie smirked at him. "Like you're a big threat."

"Enough." Mrs. Stewart, the principal's secretary, tapped her desk. "I'm sure your parents will have something to say about your behavior today. I'll take it from here, Mrs. Ruby."

A chill ran down Ginnie's spine, making her shudder.

Daddy's going to find out?

That painted the situation a different color. Suddenly the bright yellow day turned to a murky brown. Her dad, a stickler for rules, wouldn't be happy with this trip to the principal's office.

Surely, he won't punish me for protecting Toran. Daddy always says family comes first. He'll understand why I stood up for Toran. She scanned her mind for any arguments her dad would accept for her part of the fight.

The door opened behind Mrs. Stewart. Principal Reed appeared in the waiting room. His face seemed a mixture of sternness and matter-of-fact. Ginnie hoped she'd receive the "matter-of-fact" lecture. Pierce could have the other.

He called Pierce in first. Ginnie stayed in her seat, mulling over possible punishments. *Worst-case scenario, I get a day of detention. Daddy'll probably make me do the dishes for a few days, but I can live with that.*

Time moved slowly.

Staring at the clock, she flinched every once in a while as the second hand jumped around the clock face. The movement became kind of hypnotic. She closed her eyes, imagining herself in their barn at home, brushing her horse. She concentrated on the silky feel of Calliope's chocolate brown coat.

Ginnie loved horseback riding. Her earliest memories were sprinkled with hazy images of riding with her mom, just before she died, when Ginnie was three-and a-half. Mama's long curly blond hair would tickle Ginnie's cheek when they rode together.

That was pretty much all she remembered of her mom.

Anyone who ever knew her mother, Queenie West, said Ginnie inherited her mom's dark sapphire blue eyes and blonde curls. A dedicated tomboy, Ginnie wore her curls in braids because her dad wouldn't let her cut her hair.

She caught sight of Mrs. Stewart and was brought back to the present. Mrs. Stewart nodded at the clock on the opposite wall. "Mr. Reed will be with you soon."

He's sure taking a long time with Pierce. Maybe Mr. Reed realizes this mess is all Pierce's fault.

Ginnie's nerves got the better of her, making her belly clench. *Hopefully I'll only have to do an extra chore or two ... but if Dad grounds me, then it will be A LOT more chores.*

Sugar beets!

I better not get grounded over YOU, Pierce Owens!

"How'd you manage to get yourself into another boatload of trouble, Trouble?"

Ginnie jerked at the sound of Uncle Jake's voice. *How'd Uncle Jake get here so fast?* She scanned the room.

No Uncle Jake. *My mind's playing tricks on me. Of course! Uncle Jake won't let me just twist in the wind if Daddy's unreasonable.* She smiled, relaxing as she thought of her dad's older brother. *Uncle Jake will help Dad see reason.*

The principal's stern voice interrupted her thoughts. "Excuse me, Miss West?"

She stood.

Shielded behind the principal's back, Pierce sneered.

Ginnie caught herself before she returned the gesture.

Clamping her jaw shut, she forced a more pleasant look.

Just you wait, Pierce Owens. Just ... you ... wait.

CHAPTER TWO:
THE PRINCIPAL'S OFFICE

In Mr. Reed's office, Ginnie squirmed on the hard wooden chair. The principal wore a black suit and purple tie, reminding her of the men in her family dressed for church on any given Sunday morning. She peeked around. *This might not be church, but a prayer can't hurt.* She offered a silent one.

Mr. Reed cleared his throat. "I'd like to hear your side of the story, Miss West."

Ginnie sighed and told him what happened, trying to keep her voice calm, ending with: "Pierce started it. We were just having lunch, minding our own business."

Holding her breath, she searched his face and waited.

His expression held no sympathy. Mr. Reed reminded her of an eagle sizing up a tasty little mouse. "How do you think you could've handled this situation differently, Miss West?"

Wishing she could disappear into the seat, Ginnie shrugged instead. "I'm not sure. He's bigger than my brother and me. I didn't feel like I had a choice."

"You always have a choice. Next time, use your words, and get a teacher."

Fighting the urge to roll her eyes at the lameness of that advice, she turned her head and mumbled, "Oh, that'll help. But just 'til we get off school grounds."

"What was that?" Mr. Reed's eyebrows arched like an owl's.

She didn't think he really wanted an answer and she surely didn't want to give one.

He ignored her murmuring. "I'm required to suspend you for two days. Would you like to call your dad, or have me do it?"

She jumped to her feet. "Are you kidding? Pierce started it! I was just defending my brother. Can't I have detention instead? Please?" Seeing only disapproval on his face, she sank back onto the chair. *Suspended? Daddy's gonna freak!*

Trying not to moan, she didn't want to think about the mountain of chores her dad would come up with to keep her busy for the next two days.

"My dad's at work. Can I call my Uncle Ben instead?" She racked her brain for a plea that might change Mr. Reed's mind.

He lifted the phone and placed it closer to her.

Ginnie stifled the urge to fling it.

The corner of his mouth twitched. Ginnie swore he tried to hide a smile. "Pierce's parents and your father will receive a written statement of the incident. Do you have anything to add?"

She blew the bangs out her eyes. *Yeah, you're a toad, and I'm toast. This is clearly all Pierce's fault.*

Ginnie feigned a solemn look. "No, sir."

"Try harder to stay out of trouble. Your Uncle Jake always managed to find trouble when he was your age. I suggest you don't follow in his ways."

"You know Uncle Jake?"

"He was my friend in high school." *No kidding?* Something about the way he said Uncle Jake's name made her think that Mr. Reed admired her uncle. He pointed to the phone.

Thinking about her dad's probable bad reaction, Ginnie decided to plead for a different punishment. *What do I have to lose?* She took a breath and plunged ahead. "I shouldn't have egged Pierce on, but isn't there some other punishment I can do? Write a report or something?"

Mr. Reed shook his head.

Nuts! Ginnie dialed the farmhouse. The phone rang several times. She glanced at the principal.

He drummed his fingers on a pile of paper. The beat made her think of the chorus to 'London Bridges': *Take a key and lock her up, lock her up, lock her up. Take a key and lock her up …*

Uncle Ben finally answered. "West residence, Ben speaking."

Ginnie plunged ahead. "Hi, Uncle Ben, it's Ginnie. I got

suspended. Can you pick me up?"

Silence. "Why did you get suspended?"

"I got into a fight." She bit her lip. "If it helps, I won."

Mr. Reed snorted, then sobered quickly, giving her a stern shake of his head.

"What happened?" A sigh interrupted Uncle Ben's words. "Never mind. Tell me when I get there."

"Yes, sir." Ginnie cast a final pleading glance at Mr. Reed as she hung up the phone.

"I'm sorry." Mr. Reed shook his head as he smiled. It was a tight smile, lips puckered as if holding back a laugh. He leaned forward in his chair. "When we were a little older than you, Jake and I skipped school one day. Your Uncle Ben asked my folks if he could put me to work alongside Jake during our suspension."

Ginnie leaned forward, intrigued with the story.

"I didn't realize how hard farm families worked. Your Uncle Ben made quite an impression on me, in a good way. He cared enough to let us know what we did was wrong, and worked us hard enough to make me never want to repeat the experience."

She fidgeted. "My dad is exactly like him. He'll make me do the same thing." She sighed. "Can I get my books?"

Mr. Reed nodded and took a notepad from a drawer. "Take this pass, get your books and backpack, then come back here and wait for your great-uncle to arrive."

"Yes, sir." Ginnie headed for the door.

"Miss West?"

Ginnie stopped and turned. "Yes?"

He grinned. "Try to stay out of trouble. At least until you graduate from high school."

Ginnie tossed him a cheeky grin and groaned. "Yes, sir."

I'll get right on that.

Annoyed she couldn't get Mr. Reed to bend, Ginnie tried to come up with a plan 'B' to lessen the reality of dishpan hands.

The last time she got busted for her bad temper, her dad made her wash every dish in the kitchen. Another time she had to wash the hallway walls. The worst was when she had to wash the dogs and they fought and scratched and shook muddy water all over her. One had even got in a fight with a skunk and lost. *Ick!*

Glancing around the empty hallway, she considered bolting out the back way. *Yeah, that'll help … NOT!*

Her dad was a world class neat freak. Sure as shooting, he'd have her scrubbing *something*.

She took a calming breath before she entered her classroom and handed her pass to Mrs. Johnson. Her teacher gave a quick nod. "Make sure you take your science book."

Ginnie felt Tillie's sad eyes before she saw them. "What happened?"

"I got suspended for two days."

Tillie sucked in a horrified breath.

"I'm fine. No big deal." She offered a confident smile to Tillie and hugged her quickly. No matter what, she couldn't have Tillie worrying about her. Tillie worried about everything.

Right now Tillie's pet worry was getting her mom to marry Ginnie's dad. Their parents started dating last week and Tillie was waiting impatiently for them to fall in love, get engaged, and get married so that she and Ginnie could be sisters for real. Tillie's eyes widened. "What will your dad do?"

"I dunno." Ginnie shrugged. "But I saved Toran, so that's gotta count for something."

Tillie nodded. "Your dad's nice. He won't hurt you."

"Of course not. He's not like *that*." Just as the words left her lips, Ginnie wished she could snatch them back. Tillie's betrayed look plunged regret deep into Ginnie's being. She jammed her science book into her backpack. "Sorry, Tillie, I wasn't thinking."

Tillie's father had been *exactly* like *that*. Mean. He used to hurt her and her mom before he abandoned them six years ago. Ginnie slipped on her backpack and changed the subject. "See you in a couple of days. Get my homework, okay?"

"Sure. Call me?"

"If I'm allowed." She tossed Tillie her most confident grin. "Since our folks are dating, maybe your mom will help Daddy not get too mad. And don't forget … Thursday we're still going to the movies, right?"

"Yeah." Tillie's furrowed brow eased. Her smile grew.

Ginnie waved and rushed to the door.

Although she knew her dad would never, *ever*, hit her like Tillie's dad had, washing a boatload of dishes wasn't Ginnie's idea of a good time either.

CHAPTER THREE:
THE HALLWAY

Tillie finally caught sight of Toran and waited for the three seventh-grade girls to pass before she crossed the hall to meet him.

"Did you know Ginnie got suspended?" She asked quickly. Her words ran together, but she was too upset to slow down. "Uncle Ben just picked her up."

Toran adjusted his books and frowned. "It doesn't surprise me. She *did* get in a fight. Not that she *had* to."

"You sound mad at her. Why? *Pierce* started it."

"I *am* mad at her."

Surprised, Tillie locked her eyes on his. "Why? She always stands up for me. I wish *I* was that brave. Pierce is *huge*."

The deep frown on Toran's face softened. "It's one thing for her to stand up for *you*, you're a girl. I'm a guy. It's different."

"Why?"

"It just is. I gotta go." He shook his head, quickened his pace, and turned into social studies, leaving Tillie in the hall wondering what that was all about.

CHAPTER FOUR:
BACK HOME

Suspension, or not, Uncle Ben made sure Ginnie started her schoolwork as soon as they got home.

Peeking up from her science book, she smiled at three china plates hanging on the wall in front of her, decorated with playful baby goats. At either end of the plates, a glass and brass sconce held a dark purple candle.

Uncle Ben's late wife, Aunt Sadie, had collected goat and violet-themed knickknacks. She died a year before Ginnie's mom did. The farmhouse walls and shelves were dotted with paintings, knick-knacks, pillows, trinkets sporting goats and violets perched, sewn, or tole-painted on decorative plates, pillows and plaques.

When there weren't actual violets on the treasures, quite often they were in shades of purple, like the candles.

Ginnie loved Aunt Sadie's touches around the farmhouse. Even though she didn't remember her, the goats and violets seemed to be Aunt Sadie's way of saying she was still with the family, watching over them.

Her gaze shifted to an oil painting hanging over the sideboard. A young mother hugged a blond toddler son and daughter, each with armfuls of purple flowers. Daddy said Aunt Sadie bought it for Mama's second Mother's Day.

Funny how there weren't any real pictures of her mother hanging in the farmhouse. *Actually, not so funny, after all.*

Ginnie sighed and made an effort to focus on her science

homework. Just as she finished, her great-uncle brought her a ham sandwich and set it in front of her.

"Thanks. I only had a few questions in science. I don't have any other homework. May I ride Calliope?" *A ride before afternoon chores will turn this day around.*

Uncle Ben shook his head. "Your dad will be home soon. You should speak to him first, about today, before Toran gets home."

Her belly churned. *Oh yeah … Daddy. There goes a good idea.*

She glanced at Uncle Ben to see if she might be able to change his mind. He shook his head. His telepathic abilities annoyed her. "Fine. No ride. How do you do that?"

Uncle Ben laughed. "I've been an uncle most of my life. Two of my brothers gave me nephews when I was seventeen. Your grandpa was one of them. I've raised Jake and since he was a little older than you. You and he are cut from the same cloth."

Ginnie giggled at his reasoning. "Okay. I get that."

Uncle Ben nodded. "Your dad's a fair man. Tell him the truth and let's see what happens."

"Will you talk him out of a huge punishment, if he gets mad?" Uncle Ben was an even better ally than Uncle Jake, since he'd been her dad's ally since he was a kid.

"Let's see what he says first. I've been in his shoes a few times, but I've never been in yours. He loves you. That'll count for how he thinks he should deal with this. You can do the eggs with me. I'll let him know you were helpful, okay?"

"Deal." Ginnie finished her sandwich and followed him to the kitchen. She slipped onto the blue leather bar stool. "Can I candle the eggs, Uncle Ben?"

"Sure. I know you like to."

Ginnie put the first egg on the candler. She liked looking at the eggs after the candler projected a beam of light inside them to determine if there were blood spots or a growing embryo. Since there were neither in this egg, this egg passed the test. She put it on the special egg scale, weighed it, and put it in a matching-sized carton.

The younger chickens made small-and-medium-sized eggs, while older hens produced large, extra-large or jumbo-sized eggs.

Leaning against the blue bar stool back, she thought about Uncle Ben's daughter, Vi, the closest thing Ginnie had to a mom. At least until Dad made up his mind about marrying Tillie's mom, Miss Amanda. "I haven't seen Vi all week. Will she be home tonight?"

Uncle Ben shook his head. "She has a date. I doubt she'll be home before you go to bed." He set three more eggs on the towel.

"I miss her. This is how it's going to be if she marries Preston, huh?" Ginnie sighed. She put a jumbo egg in the right carton.

"Maybe not. We usually saw your folks every day." Uncle Ben added two more eggs. "Of course, your mama never got too far from her horse. We set up two cribs in what is now my room, so you two could nap and Aunt Sadie or I could listen for you while Queenie rode."

She leaned forward, eager to hear more about her mom.

"Sometimes Aunt Sadie would wake one of you up to play with you before Queenie got back."

Ginnie laughed. "Really?"

"Yes. Aunt Sadie loved babies. She couldn't get enough of you and Toran. Violet didn't come until we'd been married almost six years. Buzz came six years after that. We got custody of your dad and Jake before we had Buzz."

He set down more eggs.

"How old was Vi when Daddy came to live with you?"

"Four." Uncle Ben seemed pretty open right now.

"What were my grandparents like?" Ginnie was never sure how to act about them. They died in a car accident when her dad was eleven. She was always excited to learn more about them, until she remembered they were dead. Then she felt sorry that she never got to meet them.

"Vic was quiet, but he enjoyed playing a good prank every now and again, like Jake. Eliza hoped to be the first West to have a girl, but they could only have the two boys. Girls are rare in our family."

"That's weird, but cool." Ginnie liked having something cool in common with Vi. She would miss her when Vi got married and moved out of the farmhouse.

He nodded. "My brothers and I have thirty-nine sons and grandsons between us. Violet was the first West girl in five generations. You were the second in six. That's pretty amazing."

"Yeah, I wonder why?" The knowledge excited her, until she recalled how crazy her dad could get when he treated her like a girl instead of a tomboy. Ginnie rolled her eyes. "Do you think that's why Daddy is so protective of me? Because I'm a girl? He gets a little smothering sometimes. But maybe he'll lighten up if he adopts Tillie. Then he can worry about *her* instead of me."

"I wouldn't count on it. He loves Tillie like his own." Uncle Ben laughed and then nodded. "But dads are protective of their kids. I've always watched out for Violet. But I also look out for Jake, Buzz, and your dad as well. Doesn't matter whether they're really my sons or my nephews, they're all three my boys. That's what dads do."

Ginnie scoffed inwardly as the image of Tillie's birth father rushed to her mind. "Maybe, but not all dads are protective." She mumbled the words just loud enough for Uncle Ben to hear.

He caught her eye. "Why would you say that?"

Ginnie turned her stool toward him. "Mr. Taylor's a jerk. How could anybody be mean to Tillie? She's the sweetest person I know."

"Jasper is mostly a good man. And *his* daddy wasn't very nice."

"Why are you defending him? He's a jerk."

"Watch your tone. "Uncle Ben arched a warning eyebrow. "Jake and he were friends in high school. We spent a lot of time and effort on him. There was a time when he was a half-decent fella."

"That's hard to believe." Ginnie crossed her arms, daring him to justify his words.

"Maybe, but it's true." He set three more newly washed eggs in front of her. "Do you remember when Tillie and Amanda stayed with us those couple of weeks when Amanada first left him?"

Ginnie's mood lightened. "Yeah. We were like sisters. I wish they could've stayed."

Uncle Ben chuckled. "Some days we see Tillie almost as much. That's a good thing. Amanda has done a great job raising her. She's a sweet girl." He added more eggs to the towel and sobered his tone. "I wish Jasper realized what he threw away."

"But he hasn't been around for a while. I wonder where he's at."

"Last I heard, he was in California." He dried his hands. "The eggs are washed. How's about you just candle and I weigh and sort?"

"Sure, Uncle Ben." She enjoyed spending time with Uncle Ben so much that she startled when she heard the front screen door squeak open.

Sugar beets! Daddy's home!

CHAPTER FIVE:
DADDY'S HOME

Ginnie dropped the egg she was putting on the scale. She glanced at Uncle Ben. She knew he would let her dad deal with her. She just wished she knew whether Uncle Ben was more on her side or Dad's.

His look wavered between 'you're going to catch it now' and 'I'm right here, honey'. She tossed him a quick smile, something between 'oops' and 'how funny was that?' and exhaled a long breath.

Daddy and Uncle Jake came into the dining room, joking. "No, really?" Uncle Jake asked.

"Yes, really. I couldn't believe it," Dad replied.

Ginnie relaxed, pleased to hear the merriment in her dad's voice. She waited for him to enter the kitchen and notice her.

No sense bringing on a lecture earlier than need be.

"Hi, Uncle Ben!" Uncle Jake stopped and took a second look at Ginnie, obviously puzzled at her presence in the kitchen. "Hey, Trouble. Are we late from work or are you early from school?"

Ginnie shrugged, and turned toward the scale, the candler, and the cartons that littered the blue counter top. She put the dropped egg on the scale. It was still whole.

Dad felt her forehead. "Hi, honey. Are you okay? Did you come home sick?"

"Now that you mention it, I have felt better."

Uncle Ben cleared his throat.

Note to self, comic relief isn't a good strategy. "Sorry."

Dad's gaze moved from her face to Uncle Ben's, waiting for an explanation. When Uncle Ben didn't say anything, Dad crossed his arms in front of his chest and looked her straight in the eye. "Am I going to like what I'm about to hear?"

She turned away and studied the pot of violets on the windowsill. *Well, here comes the lecture.*

"That depends on how you feel about me getting suspended for defending my brother."

"Been there. Done that!" Uncle Jake teased.

Thank goodness for Uncle Jake!

"Hmmm. Were you hurt?" The curl of Dad's lips betrayed his stern tone.

"No, sir." She moved her gaze to the "Todd" embroidered in white thread on his dark blue work shirt.

"Was the other kid hurt?"

"Not really. But he's bigger than me and he threatened to beat Toran up just before I knocked him on his can." Ginnie sat straighter, trying to balance humility and confidence. *Surely the truth will gain me some sympathy.*

Uncle Jake didn't disappoint her. He offered her a high-five. "You knocked a bigger kid on his rear? And a boy, no less? Good for you."

Relief washed over her until Dad separated their hands.

"At least it was a boy." Dad speared Uncle Jake with a look discouraging his involvement. "But I'm thinking I'd rather you not congratulate her until I've heard the *whole* story."

Uncle Jake rolled his eyes at Dad and then winked at Ginnie.

She smiled until she caught a warning look from her male parental unit. "Serious Dad" was back in town. *Nuts!*

Uncle Ben cleared his throat again. "Jacob, maybe you ought to start your chores. I think Todd can handle parenting his child."

The "maybe" was just Uncle Ben's way of being polite. Ginnie knew he wanted Uncle Jake to stay out of it.

Uncle Jake did too, but *he* didn't seem to care. "Can I get a drink of milk first, please?" Uncle Jake begged in his best "kid voice."

"If you hurry." Uncle Ben handed him the glass he just poured.

Dad accepted a tall glass of milk as well. "Is there more to the story?"

Ginnie shrugged. "Pierce started a fight with Toran. He said something stupid, so I dissed him. Then he tried to hit Toran, so I sideswiped his foot and he fell. He was furious when he realized it was me." She offered her most innocent look. "He did look like he was going to hit Toran. I couldn't let that happen, now could I?"

Instead of responding, Dad frowned, and turned to Uncle Ben, dashing her hopes that she might win him over as easily as she had Uncle Jake.

"I presume you talked to the principal?" He drained the glass while listening to Uncle Ben.

"I did. There's zero tolerance for fighting. Both kids were suspended. If it makes you feel better, Talmadge Reed *was* apologetic about suspending her."

Dad reached for a napkin. "So he felt she was justified in this?"

"I didn't say that. He *did* say he was sorry it happened. The teacher on duty saw Ginnie flatten the other child. She didn't see anything before that."

Did Uncle Ben really have to add that last bit? Things were looking up for a whole two-point-three seconds.

"How is ol' Talmadge?" Uncle Jake reached for an apple. "I haven't seen him for a while."

So, they really were friends. Good, Uncle Jake'll help.

"Fine. How long before you take care of the livestock?" Uncle Ben replied.

Ginnie knew it wasn't intended as a question.

Uncle Jake shrugged and then grinned at Ginnie.

Dad shook his head firmly. He didn't look angry, but he didn't look happy, either. Ginnie sighed, slumped her shoulders, and tried to look more humble. "How much trouble am I in?"

"That depends on how truthful you are," Dad countered. "Who else saw it?"

"Toran, Austin, Tillie, Maddy, Levi, and Luci Jo. Oh, and Tuck." She wrinkled her nose. "And apparently a teacher or two."

Uncle Jake snorted.

Dad frowned.

Uncle Ben turned away, but not before Ginnie caught him trying to stifle a laugh.

Ginnie sucked in her cheeks.

Uncle Jake's grin revved up as Dad's smile faded. "Should I presume all your friends and your brother will back you up?"

That's a no-brainer. She flicked a blonde braid off her shoulder. "They'd better, because it's the truth."

Oops, wrong answer.

Ginnie's smile disappeared as Dad raised his finger and scowled. "Go to your room. I'll be up to talk with you after I speak with your brother. If you've left anything out, this would be a good time to remember it. Understood?" His eyes narrowed as he turned on his "lecture" voice.

Ginnie nodded. "Yes, sir. Understood."

Uncle Jake sent her a mischievous wink. He would have her back with Dad.

She stood and walked to the doorway. She bit back her desire to protest, then turned to face him. "I'm sorry I got suspended, Daddy."

"Are you sorry you got into the fight?"

"I'm not sorry I kept Pierce from hurting Toran."

Dad pressed his lips together and motioned toward the doorway again.

As soon as she passed into the dining room, she heard Uncle Jake's laughter behind her dad. "*Oh man, Todd!* How can you even *think* of getting mad at her? That was a *great* answer!"

Ginnie felt better in spite of her dread.

"Shh!" Dad hissed at him and then followed Ginnie into the dining room, pointing at the hallway in front of her. "Keep moving."

She searched his face to see if he found the situation at all amusing like Uncle Jake did.

His furrowed brow didn't bode well. He held up his pointer finger. When his eyes narrowed and a second finger went up, she picked up the pace.

"Yes, sir, I'm going." She hurried toward the stairs before he could raise a third finger.

Three fingers were *never* a good sign.

CHAPTER SIX:
THE BUS RIDE HOME

Toran felt almost happy when Tillie told him during passing period that Ginnie had been suspended.

Ginnie can't embarrass me anymore, at least not for the next two days. He dropped into his usual bus seat by the window and set his backpack on the floor.

Austin plopped down beside him.

Tillie sat in the seat in front of them. She pulled a math book out of her backpack and handed it to Toran. "I put a note in it with Ginnie's homework for tonight."

Austin intercepted the book. "Gee, I thought you didn't have to do homework when you got suspended. That stinks."

"Getting lousy grades stinks more. Our dad expects straight 'A's.'" Toran took the book from him. "Ginnie's in enough trouble for getting suspended, if she doesn't get on the honor roll because of this, she'll be in bigger trouble."

"Too bad she can't stand up to your dad like she did to Pierce. That was cool how she dumped him on his rear." Austin backhanded Toran lightly on the chest. "But she saved you."

Toran balled his fists. Fury boiled when he remembered Ginnie knocking Pierce down and the crowd laughing at her "bravery."

"I could've handled Pierce, but she didn't give me a chance. Our goat's got more sense than she does." Toran's words slid furiously into one another. "She's too stubborn for words."

Austin grinned. "I was just kidding. Lighten up."

Toran punched his right fist into his left hand. "It's not funny.

Everyone thinks I'm a sissy."

"Not anybody that matters. Huh, Tillie? We know Toran's cool."

Tillie's head popped up. "She was just looking out for you. That's what family does."

"Not in junior high. If she was my brother ... *maybe*. But she's a girl. My twin *sister* no less. I'm supposed to look out for her, not the other way around."

Austin snorted.

Anger rising, Toran locked his eyes on Austin. "What's so funny?"

"Ginnie's pretty good at sticking up for herself. I *mean, of course* you look out for her, but did you *see* her take Pierce down?" Austin elbowed Toran as he laughed. "She was *awesome*."

"*You're* not her brother. And Pierce's fight was with *me*, not her." A sick feeling swept over Toran as Austin continued to laugh. "She's a busybody."

"Austin, stop." Tillie knelt in her seat to face them. "You're making Toran feel bad."

"I don't need you protecting me either, Tillie. I can take care of myself." Toran looked out the window, pumping his foot quickly in hopes this bus ride would soon be over. *Two more stops.*

"Hey!" Austin tugged his green shirt sleeve.

Toran glanced at his best friend.

A sober look crossed Austin's face. "Why did Pierce go after you in the first place?"

Toran shrugged. "I dunno. We only have one class together."

"Why did he say you cheated? What was that about?" Tillie asked.

"I don't know. I *don't* cheat! If Ginnie had let me handle it, I might have figured it out." Toran glanced around the bus, his pulse quickening. "I guess I'll have to ask Pierce on Friday."

"Yeah, that's a good idea ... *NOT!*" Austin shook his head and pointed a finger at Toran. "You do realize that a girl half Pierce's size knocked him on his rear in *your* defense? If I were you, I'd pack my bags and get outta town. Pierce'll be gunning for *both* of you."

When the air brakes lurched to a stop, Toran almost lost his lunch. His legs wobbled as he snatched up his backpack. He had spent the day angry at Ginnie for being a busybody and himself for not stopping her. He hadn't devoted one single brain cell to Pierce seeking revenge.

Dung beetles! Ginnie, what have you gotten us into THIS time?

CHAPTER SEVEN:
AT PIERCE'S HOUSE

You got suspended over a fight *with a girl?*"

Pierce backed up, panic gripping his throat.

His father lunged at him, punching his arm with a fist.

Pierce clamped his jaw shut and bit back the pain. He hoped if he took a punch or two without bawling, maybe his father would stop hitting sooner. "I was talking to her brother. She came up from behind. It wasn't my fault."

He raised his arm to deflect the blow aimed straight at his face and stumbled backward.

Nails sliced his shoulder as his father snatched at Pierce's red T-shirt. "Are you telling me the truth?"

"Y-y-es. Of course," Pierce lied. Adrenaline forced moisture to his throat so that he could answer. "I wouldn't let no stupid girl knock me down on purpose. She snuck up on me. I didn't even touch her. It's all *her* fault."

"Then why are *you* suspended?" Hot, foul-smelling breath blasted against Pierce's cheek as he found himself pulled closer to the angry man.

Pierce tried to answer the question, but couldn't concentrate while the fabric of his collar scraped across his neck like sandpaper. "It's the school rule. Doesn't matter who's at fault."

"You musta done sumthin'! Don't lie to me, boy!" Rage flooded his father's face.

Wincing, Pierce willed himself to keep his hands down. "I'm bigger. Th-they thought it was my fault, but it wasn't." Pierce gasped for air as the meaty fist twisted his neckline, cutting deeper into his throat. "I swear. She snuck up on me. *Honest.*" His words barely squeaked out.

Blood pulsed in his ears. Dizzy, Pierce moved back in an effort to steal a breath.

His father forced Pierce's ear next to his mouth. "You better not be lying to me!"

"I'm ... not ..." Pierce croaked, eyes bulging.

With a final push away, it was all Pierce could do to stay on his feet. He steadied himself and glanced at his father, who waved his hand in a wild, sweeping motion. Trying not to cringe, Pierce swallowed again, hoping the reprieve would last.

His father let a stream of curse words flow from his lips like a river. When he dropped into his favorite recliner and picked up the TV remote, Pierce knew it would be okay to escape to his room.

Relief quickly turned to rage as Pierce shut his bedroom door. *I'll make her pay for this. If it's the last thing I do. I'll get that stupid girl.*

CHAPTER EIGHT:
THE CONSEQUENCE

G in, honey, wake up."
Ginnie felt a gentle shake on her leg. It took a second to gain her bearings. She opened her eyes.

Dad smiled at her. "Getting up early to ride Calliope before school must've worn you out." He patted her leg. "Are you awake?"

She nodded.

"Good. Toran came home."

Ginnie grinned. "What did he say?"

Toran will have my back.

"Pretty much what you said."

"So I'm not in trouble?" *Whew! Thanks, Tor!*

"I'm not mad at you. That's not the same as being out of the doghouse, though."

"What does that mean?" She cocked her head and yawned. *Toran didn't back me up?*

"It means you got suspended. Toran was certain he could've worked it out if you'd let him. You're too impulsive and I want you to give this some thought."

Ginnie frowned. "So what's my punishment?" *Toran bailed? That's not like him.*

"Punishment is such an *ugly* word. Let's use the word 'consequence' instead." He patted her leg again and smiled wider. "Discipline means 'to teach', so I've been thinking 'how do I teach you to not be so impulsive?' Then I thought of Tom Sawyer and realized an old-fashioned consequence might do the trick."

Ginnie groaned, eying him suspiciously.

He laughed.

She scowled. "So, what did you think of?"

"Whitewashing a fence. Though nowadays we use paint. The fence lining the lane needs to be painted and I think you're the right person for the job."

"Painting is my punishment?" Ginnie laughed at the verdict. "Cool! That'll be fun!"

"It's a long fence," Dad cautioned with a glimmer in his eyes. "It'll take a while."

"No prob. It'll be a cake walk."

Wow! No scrubbing anything? Awesome sauce!

"If you say so. Take as long as you need to get it done right."

"What's the catch?"

"No catch. You're grounded until it's done: no friends, no phone, and no Calliope."

"No Calliope?" Ginnie yelped, sitting straighter. "I have to exercise her. That's not fair to Calliope!"

His smile disappeared.

"Simmer down. Toran can make sure Calliope is taken care of. When the fence is done, so is your grounding. Keep complaining and I start adding days."

"Fine," she agreed, keeping her voice even. "I'll do it tomorrow, unless you have paint now."

His smile returned. "I need to buy some. Since you can't start painting yet, you can ride Calliope tonight. But that will be your last horseback ride until you've finished the fence, agreed?"

Ginnie nodded. "Agreed." She shook the hand he offered her and smiled back at him.

Painting fences? How hard can that be? Daddy's getting soft.

CHAPTER NINE:
PAINTING THE FENCE

The only time Dad made an exception to the "no-friends" part of the grounding rule was when Tillie's mom, Miss Amanda, had to be at work extra early or extra late. Today she had to go in early and Dad didn't need to be at his work until 2:00 pm.

Ginnie and Tillie walked down the lane behind him as he pushed a wheelbarrow full of paint supplies, chatting with Toran.

"Yikes. That's a long fence," Tillie said, glancing behind them down the quarter-mile lane.

"Yeah, but no big deal." Ginnie shrugged. "It's better than washing walls or dogs."

Tillie scrunched her face. "I dunno. It's supposed to be hot today."

"No prob, Dad brought a thermos of ice water. I'll paint the fence today and ride Calliope tomorrow, while *you're in school*." Ginnie wiggled her eyebrows and smiled.

"If you say so. I'd rather be in school." Tillie hugged her quickly. "There's the bus."

They hurried to catch up to Toran.

The orange-yellow school bus chugged along the road, dust swirling in its wake as it braked to a stop. Standing a few feet from the road, Ginnie and her dad watched Toran and Tillie step aboard.

Ginnie waved. "Bye, Toran! Bye, Tillie."

"Bye, Ginnie!" Tillie waved back. "Have fun!"

"Have a great day, son! You too, Tillie," Dad called.

Tillie beamed. "You, too."

Toran waved just before he disappeared inside.

The bus roared to life, spitting out its black, billowing smoke.

Dad turned to Ginnie. "Are you ready?"

"Sure! This'll be fun!" Ginnie peered at the green wheelbarrow which held a five-gallon bucket of white paint, a paint pan, two rollers, a paint brush, and a gallon of ice water.

"I'm going to help you for a while to get you farther down the lane, closer to the farmhouse. I don't want you this close to the main road by yourself."

He poured paint into the pan, soaked a roller in the white, and handed it to Ginnie.

"Okay, thanks. Then it'll go even faster."

Dressed alike to deal with the coming day, both wore blue jeans and a t-shirt--Ginnie's emerald green, her favorite color, and Dad's, a royal blue which nearly matched his eyes.

A straw cowboy hat each completed their outfits.

The humidity was manageable now, but would thicken before long. Dad pointed at the split rail fence. "Do the top rail and then the bottom one. You won't have to repaint drips that way."

Looking down their dirt and gravel lane, Ginnie could barely make out the front porch swing on their two-story, red brick farmhouse. A hammock hung between two giant maple trees to the right. It reminded her of a handkerchief.

Not quite as far, the hay barn sat to the left of the lane. Ginnie started painting. "This is fun."

Dad chuckled. "We'll see how fun you think it is when you're halfway done."

Puzzled by his laughing, Ginnie shrugged. "Did Uncle Ben make you paint this fence when you were younger?"

"Yes, but only once for punishment. Jake's done it a few times when he was in trouble."

Ginnie giggled, having no trouble picturing Uncle Jake busted as a kid. Her dad though, was a fish of a different kind. "What did you do to get busted?"

He ducked his head, acting at first like he didn't want to answer, and started painting the post. "For bickering with Jake. Uncle Ben made me do that end and Jake had to do this end. By the time we met in the middle, we decided we could be pleasant to each other."

"It's a good thing Toran and I don't bicker like you and Uncle

Jake do," Ginnie teased.

"It *is* a good thing. Uncle Ben's more patient than I am. But *your* brother is only older by five minutes and Toran doesn't pick on you."

Dad almost never scolded her and Toran, but Uncle Ben would tell Dad and Uncle Jake to mind their manners at least once a week. Ginnie loved it when Uncle Ben busted them. Always good sports, they'd exchange glances, try to look humble, and reply, "Yes, sir."

She and Toran would do their best not to laugh.

Uncle Jake called Uncle Ben 'old school'. He raised all four of his kids, including her dad, to say "Yes, ma'am," or "No, sir," and to be truthful in all their dealings. Dad expected Ginnie and Toran to speak respectfully to their elders as well, *especially* his uncle.

"True. But why do I have to do the whole thing if you only had to do half?"

"Because I didn't get suspended from school." He turned on his "lecture" voice. "You should have to work during the time you should be at school. Then the next time you think about fighting at school, you might think twice before throwing the first punch."

She shook her head hard enough to flip her braids from one shoulder to the other. "I don't care. I like painting." No way was she gonna let him ruin her good mood.

"I'm glad to hear that. You have quite a bit left to do."

They kept working. Ginnie's eyes wandered to the thigh-high cornfield in front of her. "So, Daddy, I was thinking."

"About what?" He put the roller in the paint pan.

"About something Uncle Jake said."

"Hmmm."

"The other day he said he'd best not do something or Uncle Ben would send him to the woodshed." Ginnie stopped painting to study his face. "What got you two in that much trouble?"

Smiling, Dad considered the question. "It always happened the same way: I would go along with some harebrained scheme of Jake's and we'd get caught." He stopped painting and looked her straight in the eye. "Because we *always* got caught."

She giggled. "What were the harebrained schemes?"

"I'm not telling you. Just take my word for it. I shouldn't have done what I did and I deserved what I got."

Ginnie put one hand on her hip and pointed the roller. "That's not fair. You said we should be honest with each other."

"I stand by that. I'm honestly telling you that it is none of your business to know what stupid choices I made as a kid." He pointed to the fence.

"Hmm. Well do you remember a lot about your dad? What did he do if you were busted?"

"Mostly, he'd lecture me. I didn't like him disappointed in me, so I tried to never get in trouble with him." Dad turned toward the alfalfa field behind them and stared into the distance. He seemed lost in a memory. After a moment, he shook his head and sighed. "And it wasn't until Jake and I were older that we got into any real trouble. By then we had to deal with Uncle Ben. He always gave us extra chores to do when he grounded us, so we wouldn't want to be grounded again." He grimaced and then chuckled. "And we could always expect something particularly hard or gross—he could be pretty creative."

Ginnie giggled. "What kind of chores?"

"Chopping wood, cleaning up after the animals, building cages." He stopped painting and smiled. "The worst was cleaning out the septic tank, which needed to be done every once in a while anyway, but it *always* needed to be done when we were in trouble."

"Ick, I'm glad you don't make me do that." Ginnie grimaced and finished the bottom rail. "Who got in more trouble, you or Uncle Jake?"

"Who do you think?"

"Uncle Jake, of course. But did he get in a lot more or just a little?"

"A lot more, but he didn't act out much until after our folks died." Sadness crept into his voice.

Ginnie took a step closer to him.

"When we moved to the farmhouse, we wanted to share a room and be together since we were all that we had left of our original family. But because we're so different, we bickered more and Uncle Ben got after us. Jake got mad because he didn't want Uncle Ben to be our new dad." He wiped his forehead with the back of his hand. "The first couple years here were pretty rough."

Ginnie tried to picture her dad as a young orphan boy in a new home. She had never really thought about him like that before. Sorrow burrowed into her.

"That was a long time ago." Dad sighed and pointed at the fence.

"You need to keep working. I'm glad you like painting, but you're still grounded until the fence is done."

"Yes, sir." Ginnie applied fresh paint to her roller. She wanted to learn more about Grandpa. "Do you think about your dad a lot?"

"Sometimes. But I was younger than you are now when he and Grandma died. Jake and I were lucky to have Uncle Ben and Aunt Sadie. They were very good to us."

"I'm glad you had Uncle Ben to help you—but I don't like that he gave you extra chores to do when you were in trouble, because you do that to me." Ginnie grimaced and wiped the sweat from her forehead. "But I guess that's what Opa did to *him*, huh?"

"Probably, though I can't see Uncle Ben getting in much trouble as a kid. His just older brother, Uncle Seth, on the other hand, *he* did a lot of naughty things." Dad laughed and pointed his roller at her. "Uncle Seth, Jake, you—I guess every generation needs a rabble-rouser."

Ginnie smiled as she thought of Opa, Uncle Ben's dad. She liked how he still held Oma's hand and called her 'his beautiful bride.' And Uncle Seth was always a lot of fun at family reunions.

"Jake would get in trouble for the stuff I bust you for, back talking, being defiant, and breaking rules. I pretty much only got in big trouble when I followed Jake's lead and took leave of my senses."

"And a 'for instance' would be?"

He hesitated, and then exhaled a quick breath. "All right. *One* story. One summer, Jake got this crazy idea to dye Aunt Sadie's pure white goat red for the fourth of July. So, we mixed up some cherry drink mix and dyed her, only she turned bright pink instead of red." He winked at her. "Aunt Sadie and Uncle Ben thought it was funny, but that didn't stop him from grounding us until she turned white again."

Dad glanced down the lane toward the farmhouse, then lowered his voice, like he was afraid someone would overhear. "Uncle Ben got the last laugh. We scrubbed and scrubbed that ol' goat, but she just turned lighter pink."

Ginnie laughed until her side hurt. "Seriously?"

"Yes, seriously."

"How long were you grounded for?"

"A couple of weeks. She stayed pink for months, but Aunt Sadie took pity on us."

That confession made her appreciate her dad more. He usually only grounded her for two or three days at a time.

"Now I have a question for you." Dad waited until she gave him her full attention. "Do you remember the time you filled my brand new car with water?"

Ginnie's eyes widened. "I didn't do that!"

"Oh, yes ma'am, you most certainly did. Let's move the wheelbarrow down a little and I'll tell you about it."

He's got to be making that up. But this is Daddy, NOT Uncle Jake, so maybe he's not kidding.

Curious, she followed him down the lane, looking forward to his tale.

CHAPTER TEN:
THE CARPOOL

D ad laughed as he handed her a roller. "You stuck a hose through the window of my brand new car and turned it on. It was nearly up to the seats before I figured out what you were up to!"

"No way." Ginnie sucked in a breath. "You're teasing."

"*Yes* way. I went inside the house to get a drink and got a little sidetracked. When I came back out, you were hanging on the side of my car and said 'come see'. At first I was worried that the sandals you were wearing would scratch the paint. As it turns out, that was the least of my worries."

Ginnie took a step back, not sure whether to laugh or be horrified. "How old was I?"

"About-three-and-a-half."

"I guess I was toast, huh?"

"That would be a definite 'yes'."

"And I'm still alive?"

He lifted his hat and ran his fingers through his sweaty blond curls. "Well, Uncle Ben always said God made kids cute so it increases the odds of them growing to adulthood. You put *that* theory to the test." He winked. "Of course, it didn't hurt that you looked just like your mama, the most beautiful woman I've ever laid eyes on!"

Ginnie felt her cheeks heat. "Then what happened?"

"I opened the door. The water came out like a waterfall." He gave her braid a gentle tug. "I yelled at you. Your mama came outside and laughed when you wagged your finger and scolded *me* for ruining your 'car pool'."

Ginnie giggled. "No way."

He nodded emphatically. "*Yes* way. You kept scolding, she kept laughing."

Ginnie had a hard time believing her mom was so cool about her ruining Dad's car. It made Ginnie want her more. She tried to imagine Mama standing next to her dad, chatting with her now.

Dad touched her nose. "Though to be completely fair, that mess was a little bit my fault."

"How so?"

"You overheard me talking to your mom about finding a carpool for work. Being the kind, loving daughter you are, I realized later that you were just trying to help me out."

Ginnie laughed. "It's nice to know Mama stood up for me." She pointed the roller at her dad. "If she were here, maybe I wouldn't get into so much trouble."

"If you weren't so *impulsive*, you wouldn't get in so much trouble." Dad corrected, pulling her into a hug.

"Maybe." Ginnie leaned her cheek against his chest, bit her bottom lip, and swallowed hard. "But I still wish Mama were here."

"Me too." Dad kissed the top of her head and whispered, "but she isn't, and we're doing okay."

He still sounds in love with Mama. I wonder if he's mixed up about loving Mama and Miss Amanda?

She might have asked him, but with his arms around her, and her thoughts dwelling on her mom, it was almost like being part of *their* original family again, or what she sometimes imagined it had felt like.

Ginnie didn't want that feeling to end.

CHAPTER ELEVEN: PLOTTING

A tap on the shoulder caused Toran to look up from his social studies book.

Austin stood over him. "Can you and Ginnie come over tonight?"

Toran shook his head. "Ginnie's grounded."

"Then you come over. We need to make a plan."

"About what?"

"About Pierce." Austin's voice lowered. "I'm sure he's planning revenge."

Toran's belly lurched. The same thought had haunted him for much of the day. Pierce had a reputation for holding grudges. "Let's see what's up when I get home. I have to exercise Calliope. Maybe I can ride over."

Austin grinned. "You have to exercise Calliope?"

"Yeah, but only until Ginnie gets the fence done."

"Your dad must be pretty mad."

Toran shook his head. "Not really, but it'll give me a good excuse to come over."

Austin chuckled. "You're right. See you at lunch."

CHAPTER TWELVE:
NO LONGER
HAVING A FUN TIME

The humidity was at its worst. Dad left a while ago, acting a little worn out after talking about Mama. He had given Ginnie a quick hug and said he'd bring back lunch. But all the fun of painting had disappeared when he did.

Tired and sweaty after working by herself for who knows how long, Ginnie glared at the wheelbarrow of supplies. Her energy withered with every roll. She thought about tossing the paint roller in the dirt and refusing to paint another inch.

I only defended my brother! Daddy's got to be the meanest dad in the county. He tricked me. This IS a punishment and I'm not doing it anymore.

She dropped to the ground, fuming, and rested her head on her knees, then wrapped both arms around her legs. *Mama wouldn't let him do this to me! I just know it!*

The roller bounced out of her hand when she slammed her fist on the ground. It collected grit like a magnet. She picked the rocks off until her fingers became so sticky that they were useless. Her frustration boiled. *What a mess!*

Ginnie jumped to her feet, swiping her hands at her jeans. Paint speckled rocks covered her thighs. She threw the roller down and stomped on the handle.

Glaring at the farmhouse, she broke into a fast walk, feet pounding the graveled lane. Riding Calliope would soothe her mood. She missed the feel of Calliope's velvety soft lips tickling her palm.

when she fed her an apple or a carrot. She needed to ride. A peaceful calm settled over her until she remembered Dad's words: "No friends, no phone, no Calliope." Ginnie stopped her in her tracks.

"Sugar beets!"

Whirling, Ginnie stormed toward the wheelbarrow, willing it to burst into flames. When it didn't, she kicked at the dirt. On the ground lay the blasted roller. She snatched it up and shook it at the fence.

"I'm only going along with Daddy for *you*, Calliope!" She slapped the roller against the fence, rocks, dirt and all. "If I didn't love you so much, I wouldn't do this!"

Blowing her bangs out of her eyes, she made an effort to calm down, hearing Toran's voice in her head. "It doesn't matter how mad you are, Gin, you're grounded until you do what Dad says. You shook on it."

Toran had an annoying way of being right, even when he was nowhere to be seen.

Yeah, I'm grounded for helping YOU. How fair is that?

She imagined Mama painting next to her as Dad had earlier. "You wouldn't let him make me do the whole thing, would you, Mama?"

Imaginary Mama smiled. Ginnie giggled and painted with more diligence. The painting seemed less of a punishment with Mama on her side. She began to hum.

Ginnie took a step back and glanced down the lane. She had painted herself six rows closer to the farmhouse. *Maybe Mama really is helping me out.* Ginnie smiled at the thought and scurried back to the wheel barrel and dipped the roller in the paint pan, knocking it over.

The paint spilled and pooled at the bottom of the barrel, spreading to the other brushes and the water jug. She tried scooping the paint back in the pan, but only made a bigger mess. She wiped her hands on the grass.

The leftover paint made her hands sticky. Her aggravation returned three-fold. She heard gravel crunch.

Spinning quickly, she discovered the source of her frustration, the guy she used to lovingly call "Daddy".

"Wow! You've done a lot of work! I'm impressed." His happy voice just made her madder.

She scowled. "You *knew* this was going to take forever."

He shook his head. "It won't take forever, but it may *seem* like it.

On the bright side, you have plenty of time to think about why you never want to do it again."

"You lied!" Ginnie turned away from him.

"About what? *You* said this would be a fun consequence, *I* didn't. I told you earlier I never got suspended because I didn't like painting fences."

Ginnie gestured down the lane. "But you knew I would hate it eventually, and I have to do all of it." The acres of growing alfalfa to her right went on and on forever, just like the fence seemed to.

He offered a sympathetic smile. "It occurred to me that you would be less enthusiastic as the day wore on."

Ginnie didn't miss the underlying tone – it was a sort of a teasing 'gotcha'. "On the plus side, you got farther than I thought you would."

A sparrow flew out of the field and high into the sky. *It's got freedom and I'm stuck here. No fair!* "You are a mean dad. *Mama* wouldn't make me do this!"

He pinched his lips together and let her paint in silence for a while before he spoke. "How do you know? Maybe she would have thought it up herself?"

Ginnie didn't hesitate. "No, she wouldn't!"

"Well, maybe not. But you and I have an agreement and I expect you to honor it." He pointed to the picnic basket. "I thought about having lunch with you, because we had a nice time earlier—but I think you're too angry for company. I'll fix you a plate and then leave you alone."

A soft breeze blew a wisp of hot air.

"But, I—I ..." Eating with him hadn't appealed to her at all until he said he wouldn't. Now she wanted nothing more than for him to stay and tell her more about her mom.

Sweat dripped down the side of her face. She wiped it with her shoulder, her desperation mounting. "I'm hot and tired and I don't want to do this anymore. Please, can't we make a new agreement? Pretty please?"

"No, but I understand." Dad shook his head in sympathy. "I was angry with Uncle Ben when he made me do it." He turned his attention to the basket.

Speechless, she stared as he pulled out food. Not sure how to salvage the situation, she kept working, her heart heavy as she fought off tears she didn't understand. Maybe if he saw how hard she was working, *without complaining,* he would bend a little.

"Hey, Gin! Lunch is ready."

Finally!

Taking a break and having some lunch would fix things.

She put the roller in a bag, tossed it in the barrel, and hurried to her dad. He handed her a wet washcloth to scrub the paint from her hands. After offering a blessing on the meal, Dad handed her a plate of cold fried chicken, watermelon, grapes, and her favorite chips.

She decided to invite him to lunch. "Will you eat with me? Please?"

Dad sat next to the basket and pulled out some grapes. "For a minute. Lose the attitude."

"Sorry. I just thought this would be fun ... and it was, *with you,* but it's not anymore." Her gaze dropped to his cowboy boots. "But I'm working hard—you said so yourself. Could I ride Calliope when I get half done, just once? *Please?*" Ginnie pushed her bangs out of her eyes. "You said this isn't a punishment—but it sure *feels* like it."

"I know riding soothes you, but no."

Ginnie jumped to her feet. "Why are you being so stubborn about this? I *helped* Toran. Why am I being punished at all?" Ginnie turned from him, blinking. Her tears made her angrier, but she didn't want to be left alone with her fury.

Dad sighed. "You just aren't getting it."

Ginnie pointed her chicken leg at him. "Getting what?"

"Toran's side of this." His eyes searched her face. "Ginnie, do you have any idea how embarrassing it is for a guy to have his sister beat up someone for him?"

"What's that got to do with anything?" She lifted her cowboy hat and wiped her forehead. "Toran's no fighter. He's my brother and I *always* stick up for him. Tillie too."

Dad stared at her like she had a cornstalk growing out of her head. "But Tillie's a girl."

"So? You're saying I should let Pierce beat up Toran and not Tillie? That's crazy!" Ginnie took a big bite out of her chicken leg, resisting the urge to throw it at him.

"I didn't say that. I *am* saying you should have let *Toran* handle Pierce." Dad popped a few grapes in his mouth. He offered Ginnie the rest of the bunch.

Her stomach lurched. "No, thanks."

"I think you need some space to think. I'm going to go now. I'll leave you some grapes and watermelon." He began cleaning up the lunch. "Take a break after I go to work and get out of the heat. But you're not allowed near Calliope until the fences are done."

Snap! "That's mean. Why'd you say that?"

"Because I know you won't stay away from Calliope any longer than necessary. If she's part of the deal, you'll keep going. Otherwise you'll stop and pout."

Ginnie wrinkled her nose, hating how well he knew her. "That's spiteful." She shoved a grape in her mouth before she could say anything ruder.

"No, it's motivation." He offered her a lemon-lime soda and outstretched arms. "You've been known to shoot yourself in the foot instead of getting out of your own way and doing the right thing. I don't want you to do that."

Ginnie smirked and pushed away his hands, not wanting a hug. Dad sighed again. "I love you. I even love your spirited nature ... most of the time." He took a bottle of sunscreen out of the basket. "Hold still, I'll put some sun block on your face and neck." He squirted lotion in his palm and rubbed it on her cheeks and forehead.

"I'm not a baby." Hoping to work up a "good mad," she didn't want his kindness getting in the way.

He grinned. "You're *my* baby." He added more lotion to his palm and rubbed it on her arms as well. "I need to get ready for work. See you soon."

"Will you bring back my MP3 player? It's in my desk."

"Maybe tomorrow. Today I want you to think about why you're painting the fence."

Ginnie's jaw dropped. "You're kidding me, right?"

"I'm *not* kidding. I want you to think about why you're here. Eventually you'll learn to think before you act. Being suspended isn't supposed to be fun."

"But I helped my brother!"

"Who could have handled Pierce if you'd let him."

"Have you *seen* Pierce? He's huge!"

Dad frowned. "All the more reason to use your words. You could have been hurt if the teacher hadn't been there. I know you're angry with me, but when you calm down, try to think about how you could have dealt with Pierce without using your fists. We'll talk about it tomorrow."

She crossed her arms and took a step back from him.

He blew out an irritated breath. "Take a break after I leave for work." He tipped his hat and turned from her.

Ginnie didn't offer a farewell. *Tillie thinks he's such a great dad. Wait until he busts HER for something! He should be thanking me for helping Toran, not busting me.*

Furious, Ginnie slapped the roller against the fence, not caring that it splattered her clothes. She raised her arm to toss it, but pictured Calliope before she let go.

She knew her dad wouldn't bug her about finishing the fence if she chose to take her time, but he *would* hold to the "No Calliope" rule until she did. Unless she figured out a way to change his mind, she was condemned to paint this blasted fence. "Sugar beets!"

CHAPTER THIRTEEN:
STEVE

Toran dodged students in the hall, weaving his way to the cafeteria. A boy named Steve from Pierce's class bumped into him on the way to the cafeteria.

Toran steadied himself. "Careful."

Steve guffawed. "Was that a threat? Oh wait, you wouldn't threaten me, your sister's not here to save you." With that, Steve howled with laughter and sauntered off.

Cheeks flaming, Toran glanced around the hallway. *Great! More than a dozen kids heard that. How many of them agree with him? Aw, man! You're not even here, Gin, and you're getting me in trouble.*

"Ignore him," Austin advised, then cleared his throat. "He's the closest thing Pierce has got to a friend."

Toran followed Austin to their regular table. Levi, Tillie and Luci Jo were already there. He was almost glad that Ginnie wasn't. Steve's words burned in his mind, making him even angrier with his twin. *She really knows how to mess up my life.*

"Tor, what's with the red face?" Levi asked, opening his chips. He smiled at the 'pop'.

"Nothing." Toran dropped his lunch sack on the table.

Austin chuckled. "Steve gave him a bad time about Ginnie saving him."

Toran glared at Austin. "She didn't 'save' me. She was just being herself—bossy."

"Lighten up." Austin bit his apple and pulled a chair beside Toran. "I was just teasing."

"You're not funny." Toran grabbed his lunch and left, too angry to eat. He didn't want to eat with people who thought he needed to be saved by his sister.

Lunch bag in hand, he lifted his arm, and aimed for the trash. A tug prevented the toss.

"Don't do that." Tillie shook her head and reached for the paper sack. "You have to eat. Come back. Austin didn't mean to hurt your feelings."

Toran glanced at the table he'd just left. "I'm not hungry."

"Then I'll walk with you." Tillie grabbed his hand and led him out of the cafeteria.

Steve made kissy sounds as they walked past.

Toran jerked his hand from Tillie's.

The hurt look on her face was too much for him. "I gotta go."

He rushed down the hall into the boy's bathroom and tossed his lunch in the trash on his way into the stall. The toilet overflowed and splashed liquid on his sneakers.

Can this day get any worse?

Toran spent the rest of the day avoiding Austin and Tillie the best he could.

Tillie was easier. He didn't have any classes with her. Austin gave up trying to talk to him. Out of habit, Toran sat in their usual seat on the bus. He was actually relieved when Austin sat next to him. "So, you still coming over?"

"Sure. If I'm allowed."

"Ok, then." Austin handed a piece of paper to him. "Just some ideas I had about Pierce."

Toran grinned, feeling better about the day. "Cool."

A shadow appeared before he could read Austin's note.

Above him stood Tillie, stone-faced, except for a trembling lip. *Great. Girl drama.* When his eyes met hers, she glared, turned quickly, and dropped into her seat.

His stomach clenched. "Tillie, I'm sorry." He hadn't meant to hurt her feelings, but did she have to complicate things by acting like a regular girl? Usually she acted more sensibly. That's what he needed, *two* crazy sisters.

Tillie faced slightly more away from him.

He glanced at Austin for help, but his friend only shrugged. Toran cleared his throat and tried again. "I'm sorry. I was a bonehead."

Tillie nodded and turned her head, but not before he saw the hint of a smile.

Good, she doesn't want to drag this out. "I was a bonehead *and* a jerk. Please forgive me."

It took a long five seconds for her to turn around again. "Okay. But *just* this once."

"Deal." Relief washed over him. *Maybe she's just having an off day. I sure am.*

Tillie handed him a social studies book. "There's a note inside with Ginnie's homework."

"Thanks. I'll give it to her." Their eyes met and he knew all was well.

Austin rattled the paper. "What do you think?"

"Give me a minute to look."

Toran read through the list and laughed.

CHAPTER FOURTEEN:
TORAN TAKES A STAND

Ginnie awoke, startled by three sharp knocks on her door. "Just a minute!" She peeked at her clock.

Wow! I must've been more tired than I thought.

Toran's voice rang out. "Okay. I'll be in my room."

Ginnie hurried into her sneakers. She had only planned to lie under the fan over her bed for a few minutes, before working on the fence some more. She wanted to ride Calliope as soon as she could. She turned the knob on her bedroom door, which opened into Toran's.

Their rooms used to be Uncle Ben and Aunt Sadie's master bedroom. Ginnie and Toran had shared the one room until just before their eighth birthday, when Dad and Uncle Ben built a wall down the middle. Ginnie always had to go through Toran's room to get to hers, or the stairs.

Toran stood in his room, spinning one of the many model airplanes hanging from the ceiling. Toran's passions included model cars, airplanes, and books. His tendency to inhale books helped him pass many hours on his bed or on the hammock outside, traveling through the world of his imagination as a private eye or a pirate.

Ginnie preferred her adventures in the real world, which probably explained why trouble felt particularly comfortable falling into her lap.

Glancing around her brother's room, she took note of how neat and tidy it was, as usual. No matter how hard she tried, her bed never looked as sharply made as Toran's. His light blue walls were painted with white clouds and gave the illusion of flight to the twenty plus airplanes hanging down from the vaulted ceiling.

Toran's dirty clothes basket never overflowed. His desk was empty of everything but his canister of writing utensils. His pencils always had perfectly sharpened points and his backpack hung on the back of his black desk chair, waiting to be put on in the morning.

"I didn't mean to wake you. Uncle Ben asked me to see if you were still in your room."

Ginnie shrugged, yawning. "That's okay. I need to finish the fence so I can ride Calliope. Daddy says you have to exercise her until I get it finished."

He grinned. "I know. He told me."

"Well, I'll be done soon." She rolled her eyes and smirked. "I'll get to ride her tomorrow while *you're* still in school."

"You've got a ways to go before that happens." Toran's gaze dropped. "But you wouldn't have to do it at all if you'd let *me* handle Pierce. You got busted for nothing."

"Pierce was gonna pound you! I knocked him down before he could. It *wasn't* nothing!"

"I could have handled Pierce." Toran jabbed an angry finger at her. "*You* didn't have to interfere. If you'd listened to me, you wouldn't have gotten in trouble at all!"

"You're nuts! I was looking out for you, *Toran*."

"You need a bigger vocabulary. I didn't ask for your help. You just made everything worse."

Ginnie took a step back. "Thanks for your appreciation, Victor West! Next time, I'll just remember you'd prefer a punch in the nose than my help."

"I can handle my own life." He lowered his voice, and leaned into her face. "You were *wrong*. Admit it."

"You're …" Too angry to think of an insult, she waved her brush at him, barely resisting the urge to throw it at him. Instead, she tossed the brush into her room, glared at her twin, ran down the stairs, and stormed out the front door.

CHAPTER FIFTEEN:
TORAN HELPS

Yikes, she's mad." Toran rushed to the door, determined to let Ginnie know he could defend himself against Pierce.

Uncle Ben stopped him as he reached the bottom of the stairs. "Let her calm down. She won't listen to anything you have to say right now."

Toran shook his head. "I need to fix this, Uncle Ben. She hates me. It's her own fault she got busted, but still …"

"Start your chores and let her be. She'll be calmer in a little while."

"I need to see her, *now*."

Uncle Ben arched an eyebrow and cast a glance down the lane. "If you defy me, you'll have to help her paint the fence for the next hour, but you'll be seeing plenty of her. So, think carefully about what you do next."

Toran considered his options. *Should I have Uncle Ben mad at me for disobeying? Or have Ginnie mad at me and making things worse when she gets back to school?*

Neither option appealed to him, but at least Uncle Ben knew how to behave when presented with a reasonable argument. He'd bend before Ginnie would.

"Uncle Ben, I *have* to fix this. Please let me talk to her."

Uncle Ben shrugged his shoulders and stood straighter. "I mean it, Victor West, if you walk out this door, you'll be painting the fence for the next hour." Uncle Ben gave him "the look". "Do you understand me?"

Okay, maybe he WON'T be reasonable. Now what do I do?

Remembering Steve's taunting, he decided that Uncle Ben could only make life miserable at home. He *had* to make Ginnie back off about Pierce or school would be unthinkable. "Sorry, Uncle Ben. I need to talk to Ginnie."

Strange. Uncle Ben looks almost happy.

"If you insist." Uncle Ben motioned toward the lane. "You just earned an hour of fence painting. I suggest you spend some time considering how to mind better."

"Yes, sir. I'll do that." Toran promptly forgot Uncle Ben's strange behavior and ran down the lane to catch up to his sister.

CHAPTER SIXTEEN: BRAINSTORMING

Ginnie scowled when she caught sight of her twin. "Go away!" Just what she needed: her ungrateful brother bugging her.

"I can't. I disobeyed Uncle Ben." Toran sent a wicked smile her way. "He says I have to help you to learn a lesson."

Hmmm. Ginnie laughed. "Really?"

"Really." Toran glanced at the fence. "Sorry about before. I know you had to work hard all day."

"Well, as long as you have to be here … " Ginnie handed him a paint brush. "You might as well get started. Why'd you sound so mad that I helped you?"

"Because I didn't need your help. Pierce would have backed down."

Ginnie scoffed at the idea. "In your dreams."

Toran clamped his jaw shut.

Panic washed over Ginnie. "Don't be mad at me, okay?" She hated the idea of him giving her the silent treatment, which usually followed the look he wore. "I'm tired of painting by myself. My arms ache. Friends, okay?"

He chuckled as he took hold of the roller. "Friends."

"What's so funny?"

"Uncle Ben. He said if I disobeyed him, I had to paint the fence with you. Now that I think about it, he seemed happy I stood up to him. He *wants* me to help you get done!"

Ginnie laughed at the revelation. Relief bubbled inside.

She didn't like fighting with Toran.

Toran started painting. "Austin thinks Pierce is gonna plot revenge against you for knocking him down. He wants me to come over and work on a counter plan. I have to ride Calliope anyway—so I'm going to ask Uncle Ben if I can go to his house. Don't get mad, okay?"

Ginnie nodded, realizing he wanted to include her, but couldn't. "It was Dad's idea, not yours. What kinda plan?"

Toran pulled a paper out of his back jean pocket and unfolded it. "Here."

Ginnie took it from him. She laughed as she read:

Austin's ideas:

Give Pierce a swirly
Toilet Paper Pierce's house
Fill a bag of cow manure and set it on fire on Pierce's porch
Tie Pierce to the flagpole
Give him pills to turn his pee blue
Hide his backpack
Booby trap his locker
Write a fake love letter
Photoshop a picture of Ginnie beating up Pierce and post it on Facebook
Make an announcement on the PA to embarrass Pierce

Toran pointed at the paper. "The last two are my ideas."

Ginnie handed the paper back with a chuckle. "What kind of announcement?"

Toran shrugged. "I dunno. Maybe he's wearing pink boxers with bright purple hearts on them?"

"Or he still sucks his thumb? Even better, he got beat up by a girl. We know *that's* true." Ginnie grinned at her brother, glad they had a common purpose again. "How would you get a picture of me beating up Pierce?"

"I could figure out something. But that'd make me a cyber-bully and I don't really want to do that." Toran shook his head. "But it was a good idea, huh?"

Ginnie laughed. "Yeah. A great idea, but not very nice."

"True. We could egg his place, but if Dad found out, he'd make *us* clean it up. What else?"

They brainstormed, painting as fast as they could, getting five posts closer to the farmhouse before Toran's time was up. "I could disobey Uncle Ben again," Toran offered with a grin.

"Not if he doesn't want you to," Ginnie cautioned.

It was one thing to go against Uncle Ben if their uncle didn't mind, but their dad would freak. They'd both learned a long time ago that the quickest way to get busted by Dad was to be rude to Uncle Ben. Ginnie couldn't remember ever hearing her dad back-talk Uncle Ben, even though Uncle Jake teased him on occasion.

Toran shook his head, grinning. "So I should only be defiant if he *wants* me to?"

As if on cue, Uncle Ben walked toward them. "Have you given any thought as to why you're here?"

Ginnie couldn't tell by his tone if he was messing with Toran or not, but she could swear she caught a glimmer in his eye. *Maybe he does want to help me out.*

Toran turned to him. Ginnie could tell he was trying not to smile. "Yes, sir. I realized I should listen the first time you tell me to do something. I'm sorry I didn't."

"Thank you. However, since you're finding this so amusing, maybe you should do a second hour." Uncle Ben wagged a scolding finger. "I'm not convinced you've learned your lesson."

"Yes, sir. Right after I exercise Calliope." Toran pointed down the lane. "Can I ride her to Austin's? We're working on a project. Then we can do both things at once."

Uncle Ben nodded. "Be back in an hour."

Toran waved and ran toward the barn.

CHAPTER SEVENTEEN:
TIME TO SCHEME

Austin was already on his horse, Traxx, when Toran arrived at Chandler's Crossing, Austin's family's farm.

"I thought you were never going to get here. Where've you been?"

Toran ducked his head, embarrassed. "I got busted by Uncle Ben and had to help Ginnie paint the fence for an hour. But she helped me brainstorm some more ideas."

Austin wiggled his eyebrows. "This oughta be good."

Toran laughed. "She thought we should cover him with glue and roll him around the chicken coop. He'd make a sorry mess of chicken feathers and straw, doncha think?"

"As long as I could toss a few raw eggs at him, I *really* I like that idea."

Toran nodded in agreement. "She also thought it would be really cool to tie him to the flagpole as a mucky mess for Mr. Reed to find. Only Pierce would blab and she'd get suspended again."

They doubled over laughing at the thought of Pierce tied to the pole, feathers and all.

"Let's go. I don't have long." Toran touched Calliope's ribs with his heel.

"Race you to the oak," Austin called and sped past.

Calliope caught up quickly. Traxx was taller, but Calliope was bred to race. After all, her mother was Toran's mom's National Grand Champion horse.

Toran waved at Austin as he and Calliope took the lead.

Traxx stayed neck and neck, but Calliope won by a head. Toran ran a hand down her glistening neck.

Austin groaned at his defeat. "So what do you want to do about Pierce?"

"I don't know. Everything we've come up with will earn us a one-way ticket to detention or suspension. And then my dad will come up with some way to discourage our future creativity." Toran flexed his biceps. "I only painted for an hour and my arms hurt. Ginnie's been doing it all day. Not sure I want to get suspended over Pierce."

Austin rolled his eyes. "Don't chicken out. We have some great ideas."

"Says the guy whose dad only grounds him from the phone and TV. *My* dad makes us work hard when he grounds us. Why do you think I try to avoid it at all costs?"

"It can't be that bad. Ginnie gets grounded often enough," Austin teased, lining up Traxx.

Toran chuckled. "She's something else. Uncle Ben says smart people learn from their own mistakes, wise people learn from other people's mistakes. I'm not sure *she* learns from anybody's."

"She's smart *and* a smart aleck." Austin shook his head and laughed. "I *like* that about her."

"I like the idea of busting Pierce without doing time myself. How can we set him up and still look innocent?"

"We could ring and run Trixie's patties."

"How are we going to get to Pierce's? He lives next to the school."

"The horses?" Austin stroked Traxx's neck.

"Yeah, right." Toran shook his head. "My dad would never go for it. Your house is as far as he lets us go."

"My brother then. Pete Jr. has his license. He's always in for a good prank."

"Now you're talking." Toran offered a high-five. They schemed for a few more minutes before Toran had to leave.

"I'll call you after I talk to Pete. I'm sure he'll be okay with driving."

"Cool. I'll tell Ginnie." Toran waved goodbye to his friend and tapped Calliope with his boot heel.

CHAPTER EIGHTEEN:
UNCLE JAKE

Ginnie walked along the lane with Dad to where she'd left the wheelbarrow parked the night before. He whistled his approval. "Wow. You got pretty far along."

"Can I have my music today?" Ginnie asked, picking up the rollers.

He opened the paint bucket. "Maybe. What did you think about while you painted yesterday?"

Ginnie grinned. "After I got over being mad at you because you tricked me?"

"Yes, *after* that would be good." Dad chuckled. "But I did try to warn you this would be a bigger job than you thought."

"You didn't very hard." She caught herself before she rolled her eyes at him, not something that made him happy.

He cleared his throat and arched a warning eyebrow.

She glanced at the fence. "Sorry." She sorted through a few responses before finding one that he would probably accept in answer to his question.

"Toran thought it didn't need to happen, but I knew Pierce would hurt him. So I protected him." Ginnie searched his face for approval. "But if I waited, maybe I wouldn't have needed to."

He nodded at her. "You're getting a lot closer to what I wanted you to come up with."

"Close enough to listen to my music while I finish the fence?"

Dad shrugged. "Maybe. Think a little harder. It has something to do with your brother."

Ginnie grimaced. "What about my brother?"

Dad's raised his pointer finger.

"Sorry. But *I* got in the fight, not him."

"Bingo!"

Huh? "I don't get it."

"Think harder." He filled the paint pan and put the lid back on the bucket.

What does he want me to say? "But Toran didn't get in a fight."

Dad smiled. "Exactly."

"Are you saying I should've let Pierce beat up Toran?"

"No, I'm saying it wasn't your fight in the first place. I know *you* think you need to protect Toran, but *I* think Toran can look out for himself."

Ginnie kicked the dirt. "You made me paint this dumb fence because you didn't think I should help my brother? What happened to putting family first? That's pretty lame."

"No. What I want you to get from this is that maybe he doesn't need you to take care of him as much as *you* think he does. That's all I'm saying. Okay?"

"Got it. Can I have my music now?" Ginnie asked, not even bothering to mask her irritation.

"Ask me after you've lost the attitude." His tone matched hers. He turned and left.

Ginnie kicked the wheelbarrow and dropped to the ground. She was working up another "good mad" ... until she thought about Calliope. She groaned as she stood, and began to paint. She was so focused on her thoughts she didn't hear Uncle Jake come up behind her.

"Hey, Trouble, you got another roller?"

Ginnie whirled to find an amused Uncle Jake. "Sorry to startle you. I wasn't sneaking."

Her heart raced. "Yeah. But Daddy's mad at me again. You probably shouldn't help."

"I know. Geez, Gin! You really know how to push his buttons!" He grinned and picked up a roller. "But I want to help anyway."

Ginnie planted a hand on her hip. "*You* push his buttons, too."

He tweaked her nose. "True—but I'm bigger than he is and he can't ground me."

Ginnie smiled and took a second look at him. With his cowboy hat on, he resembled her dad. Their faces were the same square shape, with a strong jaw. Although Uncle Jake's coloring was all around darker. His eyes were a deeper blue and his hair a slightly wavy, medium brown. He also had a bronzer tan.

"If Dad comes, will you keep him from busting me?"

"I'll do my best." Uncle Jake pointed down the lane. "Scoot over so he sees you first."

They worked quickly, joking and teasing, knocking off four posts and the railings in between before Uncle Jake quit. "I'd help more, but they'll be done with the eggs soon and I don't want you in more trouble with my brother. Besides I can handle Todd, but Uncle Ben still scares me."

"Really?" Ginnie cocked her head to the side.

"No." Uncle Jake shook his head and laughed. "He tries to be fair. As long as you're not being *too* big of a smart aleck, he's easy to get along with."

"I know. My dad's like that."

A black and orange butterfly landed on the fence. It fluttered its wings three times and then flew away.

"I'm glad he's my younger brother and not my older one. Between you and me, he tends to nag a little too much."

Ginnie rolled her eyes. "No, really?"

"Speaking of smart alecks." Uncle Jake reached over and pushed her hat further down on her head. "I better go. Our benevolent dictator will be wondering where I am. Good luck!"

He made it halfway between Ginnie and the end of the lane before Dad appeared. Ginnie sucked in her breath as Dad greeted Uncle Jake. *Oops!*

CHAPTER NINETEEN:
DONE WITH THE FENCES

D id you have a nice visit with Uncle Jake?" Dad asked. Ginnie glued her eyes on the fence and painted. "He was keeping me company."

"That's what *he* said. How much painting did he do for you?"

Ginnie held the roller mid-air. "Who said he did any?"

He chuckled. "Me. He has a soft spot for you. He helped you, didn't he?"

After studying Dad's face a moment, Ginnie decided it was in her best interest to make an admission. She nodded.

"I didn't hear you." His "lecture" voice startled her. He knew she hadn't said anything.

Ginnie's heart skipped a beat. She let her gaze drop to his dusty leather cowboy boots and swallowed hard. "Yes, sir, he did."

He peered at her a few seconds before he laughed. "You considered denying it, didn't you?"

Ginnie's cheeks heated.

"What made you change your mind?"

She shrugged. "If I lied, you would probably know. It's not worth the trouble."

"Good answer. Here." He handed Ginnie her MP3 player.

"Cool. Thanks."

"You're welcome. You're coming along nicely. Maybe you're getting too much help? I do want you to learn something besides painting a fence."

"I know. Quit being impulsive. Right?"

He nodded. "I'll help for a few minutes."

She smiled. "Did Uncle Ben help you out when he told you to paint the fence?"

"The second day, when I answered his questions the way he wanted me to." He raised his eyebrows playfully and returned her smile.

"Hmm. I kinda figured. He was a pretty smart dad, huh?"

"He's *still* a smart dad." They knocked out two posts and the rails in between.

Ginnie stopped painting. "Did Uncle Jake admit to helping me?"

"No, but I figured he had. You got pretty far along from where you were. I'll pour more paint. Only six more posts. You might get done before I go to work."

"Maybe, *if* you keep helping me."

"I've helped you a lot. See ya!" He kissed her forehead. "Oh, and keep drinking!"

"Yeah, yeah, yeah." Ginnie put her ear buds in and turned on her music.

Three huge shade trees grew in a cluster not far from her, at the end of the lane. It wouldn't be long before she could enjoy their shade. A small flock of five white ducks quacked and splashed in the brook running parallel to the gravel and fence.

Smiling at the scene, Ginnie wished she could join them. She wiped her forehead with the back of her hand and decided to take a break after she finished the next post. *Only four posts to go.* After putting the roller in a bag, she went inside to see if there was any iced peppermint tea left.

Uncle Ben poured her some and gave her a snicker doodle as well. "Are you about done?"

Ginnie gulped the rest of her tea. "Daddy helped and so did Uncle Jake."

"That's what Todd said." He looked her straight in the eye. "He also said you considered lying about it. Don't ever lie. At the end of the day, you only have your knowledge and your word. Make sure they mean something.

"Yes, sir. I owned up—I didn't want Daddy mad at me. I'm almost ungrounded."

Uncle Ben sat on the barstool next to her. "You know, keeping your dad happy is a good reason to do the right thing, but it isn't the *best* reason. You should choose the right because it's the right thing to do. And it's always better to own your behavior, good or bad." His voice softened as he handed her another cookie. "You have to face yourself in the mirror. Make sure you can look yourself in the eye."

"Yes, sir." Ginnie blew her bangs and nodded.

"And if you can smile when you look, it's even better," Dad added as he came into the kitchen. He winked at her. "That's what Oma would say, when Opa gave us that lecture."

"It's timeless advice. I heard it all my life and it's my duty to pass on the wisdom of my elders. Yours too, Todd Benjamin West," Uncle Ben scolded, a small smile lighting on his lips.

"I didn't poke fun, *Uncle* Benjamin." Dad's playful tone made Ginnie giggle. "I passed on the wisdom. You skipped part of the lecture, so I finished it. Isn't that my duty as her dad?"

Uncle Ben cleared his throat and straightened. "You spend too much time with your brother."

"You're the one who insisted we had to get along. Sorry it backfired on you."

Ginnie stifled a giggle, wondering what happened to her dad. The man in front of her could be Uncle Jake's blond twin.

Uncle Ben wagged a teasing finger. "Just for being cheeky, you should help Ginnie finish the fence."

Dad shook his head. "I wasn't cheeky. I told the truth, just like you told my daughter to."

Ginnie laughed and popped her hands over her mouth.

Dad sent a playful glare her way. "You set me up!"

"No, she didn't." Uncle Ben shook his head, his gray-blue eyes twinkling. "You did that yourself by being a smart aleck. Help her finish up and I'll get you both a bowl of ice cream when you're done."

Ginnie and Dad looked at each other, raised their eyebrows, and exchanged smiles.

"Yes, sir," they replied together.

All three of them laughed.

Uncle Jake came into the kitchen. "If I help, do I get ice cream?"

Uncle Ben sized him up. "Were you eavesdropping?"

"Absolutely! It isn't often that my perfect little brother smarts off." He locked his merry eyes on Uncle Ben's. "I wanted to see if you'd nail *him*, like you do me. Glad to see you don't always play favorites."

"I don't *ever* play favorites. I love you both and you *know* that. But I don't have a lot of patience for smart alecks and *that* isn't news to either of you."

"Yes, sir," Dad and Uncle Jake replied together, rolling their eyes at each other.

Ginnie's mouth dropped in surprise. Dad scolded her quite often when she rolled her eyes at him. Sometimes it made him downright angry.

He caught her gaze and ducked his head. "Come on, Gin. The old man has spoken." Dad winked at her. "See? I told you I get in trouble when I follow Jake's lead."

He ducked as Uncle Jake pretended to throw a punch.

"Hey, hey! Jacob! You know I don't allow brawling in the house. Go help your brother!"

Uncle Jake snorted. "Aw man, Todd! You got me in trouble too. I was actually looking good to the old man. Too bad it didn't last more than a minute."

Ginnie giggled. "You guys are too funny."

Uncle Ben shook his graying head. "They're too *something*, but funny isn't the word coming to *my* mind."

"Come on, Trouble. We'd better get going. See ya, Unca Ben." Uncle Jake led the way out the side porch door.

Ginnie tagged both men and sprinted ahead.

They chased after her, passing her easily.

She had almost caught up to them when they reached the wheelbarrow. "Almost!" she gasped.

They laughed. Dad handed her a roller. "You cheated."

Ginnie grimaced. "Your legs are longer. You're a dad, you shouldn't be so fast."

"What does that have to do with it? Being a dad doesn't hinder my ability to run."

"It should. You're old," Ginnie complained.

Oops! That was the wrong thing to say.

Uncle Jake roared with laughter.

Dad scowled. "Would you like to finish painting by yourself? I'm not old. I'm in my prime, thank you very much." He pointed an indignant thumb at his chest. "Besides, I beat you *both* and Jake's older than me."

"Two years, big deal," Uncle Jake retorted. "I let you win. I didn't want to make you look like a wimp in front of your kid." He winked at Ginnie.

"He missed the lecture on always telling the truth. Do you want to give it?" Dad joked.

Uncle Jake picked up a roller. "No thanks, I've got it memorized."

"Hmm, three people, two rollers. You guys don't need me." Ginnie took a step backwards.

Uncle Jake dropped the roller, picked Ginnie up, and flipped her upside down. Her cowboy hat fell off. "Not so fast! Look, Todd, two paintbrushes." He made Ginnie's braids weave back and forth. "And the paint almost matches her hair color. Cool huh?"

Dad picked up a braid and examined it. "Hmm. Not very sturdy. But it'll work."

"Don't you dare! I'll tell Uncle Ben." Ginnie tried to climb up her uncle and right herself. It didn't work. She folded her arms across her chest and tried to look stern.

"You have to *get* to him first," Dad cautioned, the teasing glimmer back in his eye. "And when it comes to you, *I* outrank *him*. So I'm not sure how much good tattling would do ya."

Ginnie rolled her eyes. "Yeah, yeah, yeah!"

"Stop that." He motioned to Uncle Jake to set her down. "She's turning red, Jake, flip her over." Dad handed Ginnie her hat once she stood on her feet. He pulled Uncle Jake aside, whispering something in her uncle's ear.

Ginnie couldn't catch their words.

"That's fine. I don't care," Uncle Jake said.

They walked over to her. Dad looked at Ginnie. "Go get Calliope and ride. We'll finish up, but you get to finish the laundry today, deal?"

"For reals?" Joy and disbelief radiated through her entire body. "Awesome sauce!"

"Yes, for reals. You painted nearly a quarter-mile of fence and gave me very little attitude. You've handled yourself well." He hugged her. "Enjoy your ride."

"Thanks, Daddy!" Ginnie squealed and then hugged her uncle. "Thanks, Uncle Jake!"

"No prob. Uncle Ben has a soft spot for girls. That's why he busted *us*. Go have fun."

Dad shoved a roller at Uncle Jake. "That's not true. Quit lying to my child!"

"I don't believe that, either." Ginnie shook her head, glancing from her uncle to her dad.

"You don't think he didn't feel sorry for her? He didn't make sure I had a lot of help when he made *me* do it," Uncle Jake insisted.

"Because *you* were a glutton for punishment. Even when he busted you for smarting off to him, you'd keep sassing. I was there. I remember."

"*Whatever.* Ginnie, go ride." He waved her away and turned to Dad. "You and I have time to argue about it."

"Good luck with that. You were a hardheaded kid. That's the truth, so there's nothing to argue about."

Ginnie left before she could be asked to take sides. She was out of the doghouse with her dad and didn't want trouble with her uncle.

It didn't take long to saddle Calliope and be on her way.

Now that she was done with the fence, she needed to concentrate on how she was going to handle Pierce when she went back to school.

CHAPTER TWENTY: LUNCH

Lunch in the cafeteria was quickly becoming unappetizing.

The more Austin bugged Toran about seeking revenge on Pierce, the sicker Tillie felt. Her belly churned, hating the tension, the chaos, and the light-heartedness of Austin's plans. They weren't the least bit funny to her.

The half-eaten bologna sandwich lost its appeal.

Glancing around the table, her stomach roiled more as her friends laughed and congratulated Austin on his latest idea to pay back Pierce or rather, his idea to "help motivate Pierce to leave Ginnie and Toran alone."

Maddy and Luci Jo giggled while Levi kept trying to one-up Austin's ideas. Toran acted interested. He usually had more sense, but even he wasn't objecting to Austin's crazy talk.

It felt wrong to plot against Pierce, even though Tillie didn't like him any better than the boys did.

There was something about Pierce that was vulnerable in spite of him being a bully. Not that she could ever be friends with him, he scared her too much.

But still … Austin didn't understand and Tillie couldn't form the words, even in her mind, to explain it to him.

She rarely saw Pierce at ease with a group. He usually kept to himself, unless he wanted something. Then he was rude and demanding.

Most people usually just gave Pierce whatever he wanted in hopes he would just leave them alone.

Toran, Ginnie, Austin, and herself were the 'Four Musketeers'... more like family and friends all mixed together. Tillie liked Maddy, Luci Jo, Tuck, and Levi, but they were "school" friends.

After all, if Ginnie's dad would hurry up and fall super in love with Tillie's mom, Ginnie would be her 'for real' sister and Toran would be her brother.

Tillie grimaced at the thought.

That would be awkward, but she'd deal with it. She often thought that Toran would be the man she wanted to marry when they grew up, but maybe that was because he was so much like his dad. Kind, safe feeling, strong, and ... and he was cute, *super* cute ... *and* he didn't even know it.

"What's so funny, Til?" Toran asked.

Tillie's cheeks flamed. No way was she admitting to her thoughts on his cuteness. "Nothing."

"Come on, admit it. You think sneaking into Pierce's house and tying all of his clothes in knots would be hysterical," Austin insisted, laughing an obnoxious laugh that Levi echoed.

"In what world?" Tillie stood, angry. "Pierce's mean enough without you giving him a reason to be meaner. When people are mean—you treat them like snakes and stay away, 'cause if you don't, you'll get bit!" She threw her lunch in her bag. No way could she eat another bite.

As she whirled away from the table, Toran moved in front of her, blocking her way. "We were just kidding. It was a dumb idea. Stay."

"No, it wasn't!" Austin protested.

"It's against the law." Toran speared him with a smirk. "It's called 'breaking and entering'. It *was* funny, but it's also impractical."

"You can quit talking like an old mother hen now." Austin shook his head and packed up his own lunch mess. "And it *was* funny."

"Whatever." Toran turned back to her. "Tillie, we're not gonna do it. We're just joking. You're right." He cast a warning glance at Austin. "It's not a good idea to poke a snake with a stick."

The nods and apologetic smiles of the others, calmed the knots tightening inside Tillie.

"Besides, Austin's all talk. No way would he take on Pierce at his place," Levi teased.

Austin pushed his chair away from the rectangular table. "I took on Pierce right here, next to Ginnie and Toran. *You* didn't, so shut up already."

The knots tightened again.

"I was gonna. But everything happened so fast. And Ginnie didn't need my help, or *yours* either," Levi said in a mocking tone, rising slowly from his chair.

Toran fisted his hands, then pointed a finger at Levi. Before he could say a word, the bell rang.

Tillie gently pushed his hand down. "We need to go."

They locked eyes. Toran's jaw tightened. He clamped his mouth shut, nodding. He pushed his chair against the table and motioned for Austin to back up.

Silently, they filed out. A look of bewilderment crossed Levi's face.

Austin slammed his chair against the table and snatched at his trash, crushing it in his hand.

Nothing was funny anymore … to any of them. The familiar anxiety Tillie tried so hard to keep at bay burrowed through the knots, twisting and tightening until she could hardly breathe.

CHAPTER TWENTY-ONE: THE WALK

Ginnie met Toran and Tillie at the bus stop at the end of their lane, anxious to know how their day went.

"Fine, no thanks to you," Toran grouched.

Ginnie locked her eyes on his. "What's *that* supposed to mean? I was home all day. How can *your* bad day be *my* fault?" She rubbed her aching arms and turned to Tillie. "What's his problem?"

Tillie shrugged. "Austin teased him about you saving him from Pierce."

Ginnie's belly did a flip. "How is Pierce?"

"Suspended, just like you." Toran adjusted his backpack and stormed off.

"Oh, yeah. I forgot he's at home too. I'll bet *he* got to watch TV for his two days." Her arms ached even more as she thought about it. "But at least the fence is done. I got to ride Calliope a couple times today."

She kept in step with her brother and friend.

"Is your dad home?" Tillie asked.

"Nope, he's working."

"Nuts."

"Why?"

"I was hoping we could go out as a family today or at the very least he'd take my mom out for dinner. They need to hurry up and fall in love so they can get married."

Toran laughed. "He likes your mom just fine. Don't worry. But they've only been dating officially for four days. Give them a little more time. He's not likely to change his mind already."

"Yeah, especially since it literally took him years to get around to asking her in the first place," Ginnie agreed.

"It's not funny." Tillie's hands flew to her hips. She stopped walking. "You guys have each other. And Uncle Ben, Vi, Buzz, your dad, and Uncle Jake. I only have Mom and I hate our apartment. I'd rather be here, at the farm."

So much for friendly conversation.

"Well, you're here most of the time anyway," Toran said, and started walking again. "And since you are, let's get the chores knocked out. Buzz gave me a game for my new computer. It's a *two-player.* We have to defeat some aliens and save the planet. You'll love it."

Tillie grinned. "Cool. Sounds fun."

"Yeah, sounds fun," Ginnie echoed unenthusiastically, not liking how Toran put the emphasis on "two-player". Toran usually included her in everything.

Tillie threw an arm around her and smiled invitingly. "We'll take turns."

Toran tensed his jaw and looked straight ahead.

At least TILLIE knows how to treat a sister.

CHAPTER TWENTY-TWO:
MISS AMANDA

When Miss Amanda picked Tillie up after work, Uncle Ben invited her to stay for dinner. Ginnie paid extra special attention to everything she said and did.

She liked how Miss Amanda hugged Tillie, and then took a minute to hug and address Toran and herself as well. Ever since Dad and Miss Amanda started dating officially, Miss Amanda was even nicer to her than usual.

Today, Ginnie held her a little longer than normal, enjoying the smell of her perfume. She tried to imagine Mama hugging her instead of Miss Amanda, but couldn't. When Miss Amanda laid her chin on the crown of Ginnie's head and squeezed her more firmly into a hug, a warm feeling cascaded over her, comforting her like the drizzle of a much awaited shower.

She glanced up and took note of Miss Amanda's caring green eyes. "Is everything okay, Gin?"

Embarrassed, Ginnie nodded. "My arms still hurt from painting the fence."

"I guess they would be, that's a lot of work." She offered a sympathetic smile. "I bet Uncle Ben has some ointment for sore muscles. I'll rub it on your arms if you like."

The idea appealed to her on the one hand. *I guess that's what moms do.* On the other, she didn't want Miss Amanda to fuss over her. She must have hesitated too long, because Miss Amanda took her by the hand, led her into the kitchen, and asked Uncle Ben for some ointment.

Uncle Ben rummaged through the medicine cabinet and produced a white tube with a picture of a sun,

"Thank you." Miss Amanda took it from him and proceeded to rub iridescent white goo on Ginnie's arms.

Soothing warmth saturated her skin. The strong medicine-y smell assaulted Ginnie's nose, but Miss Amanda's gentle fingers made her forget the insulting fragrance almost immediately.

Vi often took care of her like this, but somehow, it felt even nicer for Miss Amanda to do it. "Better now?"

"Yes, thanks." Ginnie was amazed at how much better she felt, not sure that the medicine had much to do with it.

After dinner, Ginnie was sorry to see Miss Amanda go. She held on a little longer when she offered a good-bye hug. "Toran, Ginnie, don't forget. Tomorrow's a teacher work day and I'm picking you up for the movies. Be ready please, since I'll be on my lunch hour." Miss Amanda opened the door to her silver-blue car.

"We'll be ready," Toran assured her.

Ginnie nodded. "Thanks. See you tomorrow."

"See ya." Tillie got into the passenger side.

Ginnie watched them back up and turn toward the dirt and gravel lane. About half-way down, the car was obscured by the growing cornfield.

She sighed, realizing that today she was sadder at seeing Miss Amanda leave than Tillie.

CHAPTER TWENTY-THREE:
THE MOVIES

S tanding in line at the concession stand, Ginnie, Toran, and Tillie bought a large drink, jumbo popcorn, and some chocolate covered raisins to share.

"We have enough money for another drink and candy for the next movie," Toran said, handing Tillie the large soda. "We get free refills on the popcorn."

"How about gummy worms ..." Tillie's voice trailed off as she turned. "Uh-oh."

Ginnie followed Tillie's gaze to the lobby door. Her body shuddered when she saw Pierce Owens walk through the glass doors. *Great! If I get into another fight with Pierce, Daddy's gonna skin me alive.*

She blinked, hoping he would just disappear.

No such luck.

Once he spotted them, Pierce made a beeline their way. His scraggly brown bangs reached his narrowing blue eyes. He stood almost a head taller than Ginnie and twice her size around.

"I was hoping he'd let that fight at school go," Tillie whispered. "But he still looks kinda mad."

Ginnie didn't miss the quiver in Tillie's tone. "I bet he spent his two days playing video games." She rubbed at her arm, her muscles still protesting the hours of painting.

"Just drop it, Gin." Toran stood in front of her, blocking Pierce's path. "Dad might decide the fence looks better blue if you get into it with him again."

Onward Pierce strode, moving like a tank, determined and straight ahead, not stopping until he stood directly in front of them. With a snarl glued to his face and his eyes narrowing to slits, he raised his fisted hand menacingly. "I hope you've got a cell phone, 'cause you're going to need it to call a waaahmbulance!"

"Oh please, like you could hurt me!" Ginnie snapped.

He edged closer.

Ginnie started to rethink taking him on. He didn't seem quite so big three days ago at school.

Toran turned to her. "Don't let him get to you."

"Yeah--don't let me get to you!" Pierce echoed and then pushed Toran hard enough to make him stumble.

"Get your filthy hands off my brother!"

So much for ignoring Pierce.

Ginnie grabbed for the bully's hand.

He kept it out of reach.

Tillie stepped between them, pulling Ginnie's arm. "Come on. Don't let him ruin our day.

"Mind your own business!" Pierce bared his teeth like a savage dog. He grabbed Tillie's arm, made her whimper, and spilled the soda to the floor.

Tillie's free hand flew up and her eyes squeezed shut as if waiting for a blow. The color drained from her face. Peach became cream, then a sickly white. Ginnie knew why. Tillie had suffered at her father's hands before he left his family six years before.

"Let go of Tillie!" Ginnie demanded.

"Make me!" Pierce spat.

Toran moved in front of her. "Let me handle this."

"No way!" Ginnie bobbed, keeping her eye on the bully. "Pierce, go away!"

He let go of Tillie and leaned in closer to Ginnie. "You and I are going to settle this once and for all!"

"I've already knocked you on your rear. I think it's settled," Ginnie retorted, spite staining her tone.

Pierce growled.

"Just walk away," Toran told Pierce.

"Why don't you make me?" Pierce invited, cocking his head in a mocking way. "Oh yeah, that's right. You have your *sister* do all your fighting for you."

Toran's face flamed red. His jaw clenched tight.

Pierce pushed Toran again.

Ginnie punched Pierce in the stomach. One fast hit, right on. Pierce lost his breath.

"Leave him alone!" Toran snapped at Ginnie. His gaze flew to Pierce. "Your fight is with *me*, not my sister!"

"It's with both of you, *now*." Pierce stood straight. He pushed at Toran, who took a swing at Pierce's face.

Pierce ducked slightly.

Toran's punch glanced off Pierce's cheek.

Pierce chortled. "You're pathetic!"

Toran didn't miss the second time, landing his fist in the middle of Pierce's belly. When Pierce bent forward, Toran brought his knee up, catching Pierce in the face.

Only grunts and groans came from the almost down and out, Pierce. Ginnie pushed at the bully.

Tillie pulled at Toran.

Pierce swung his fists as hard as he could, like an out-of- control windmill.

Ginnie maneuvered herself behind Pierce. With a slight kick of her foot and a cloud of raining popcorn, she had Pierce off balance before he knew it. Down he fell!

Knocked on his rear for the second time.

Pierce's face turned purple. His fury overflowed.

"I told you to let *me* handle him!" Toran snapped.

Pierce jumped to his feet. His eyes pierced Ginnie's. "I'm going to pound you!"

Ginnie raised her arm to ward off the blow, adjusting her feet to brace for it.

An onlooker grabbed Pierce's arm before he could strike. "Whoa, Bud! You're not hitting a girl on my watch. She's half your size." The stranger held him firmly as Pierce tried to wrestle himself from the hold. "Everything was fine until you showed up."

Pierce continued to thrash as Ginnie backed away.

Toran gestured for Tillie and Ginnie to keep moving.

"Let go of me!" Pierce thundered.

"As soon as you apologize to the young lady for grabbing her arm."

Wow! That man is HUGE!

"Sorry!" Pierce snarled, not at all apologetic.

Tillie nodded, still pale.

"You three go ahead." The man tightened his grip as Pierce lunged for them. "I'll make sure he doesn't bother you."

"Thank you, Mister!" Toran motioned for the girls to go ahead. A concession clerk handed Toran a fresh tub of popcorn and cup of soda.

"Thank you!" Ginnie and Tillie echoed, moving past Toran. Tillie's voice shook.

Toran handed Ginnie the soda and took hold of one of Tillie's arms as Ginnie grabbed the other. Tillie's whole body trembled. She seemed barely able to put one foot in front of the other.

"Are you okay?" Toran whispered.

Nodding, Tillie smiled her gratitude, still pale.

When they reached the theater Ginnie burst out laughing, relief causing her whole body to feel weak. "Did you see Pierce's face? His eyes were like jumbo-sized eggs!"

"I'm just glad that man was there!" Tillie said.

"Me too!" Toran agreed.

Both offered Tillie a sympathetic smile.

When the movie started, Ginnie watched the comedy, occasionally glancing around the theater, making sure Pierce didn't show. Tillie seemed distracted. Ginnie and Toran sat on either side of her. As the movie continued, Ginnie laughed along with the punch lines.

They bought more candy as they waited for the second movie to start. Tillie handed Ginnie the popcorn bucket. "Maybe he went home."

"I hope so." Toran said and plucked a few napkins from the holder.

Ginnie shrugged and hoped Tillie was right.

The second movie wasn't as funny, because it had a big dumb boy in it who reminded Ginnie of Pierce. She gave school a quick thought, hoping tomorrow wouldn't be a problem.

CHAPTER TWENTY-FOUR:
AFTER THE MOVIES

The sun hung high in the sky when Miss Amanda dropped them off in front of the red brick farmhouse. Ginnie and Toran arrived just in time to start their afternoon chores.

Only Uncle Ben's truck and Dad's hunter green sedan sat in their parking spots. Dad and Uncle Jake would be arriving home soon in Uncle Jake's truck.

A slight breeze picked up. Once Miss Amanda and Tillie pulled away, Ginnie made sure she and Toran were still on the same page about the fight at the movies. "We're not telling Dad about Pierce, are we?"

"Are you nuts? It would only worry him and he can't change anything." Toran pointed at the lane. "And I've had enough of painting fences for a while. We'll each be given an end, and an order to meet in the middle."

"Ahhh, and I was just thinking it'd look good painted blue." Ginnie pulled strands of hair from her eyes. "Let's do our chores and see if we can ride Calliope to Austin's."

Toran opened his mouth and then shut it. He blew out an impatient breath. "Okay, beat you to the barn," Toran called ... after he got a head start.

"Cheater!" Ginnie protested, then chased after him.

He kept running. Ginnie nearly caught up to him when he ducked into the barn. She followed him to the pet feeders.

Uncle Jake's black hunting hound, Bandit, jumped up on Toran. "Down boy. I'll get you some fresh water, hold on."

Bandit licked his hand and then sniffed at Toran's ankles. Toran scratched his head. "Good boy, Bandit."

Ginnie filled the cat feeder while Toran freshened the water bowls. When he finished, Toran cleared his throat. "Ginnie?"

"Yeah?" She pushed the lid down on the cat food container.

"You've really got to leave Pierce to me."

"Why? You're no fighter."

His eyes narrowed. "Neither are you."

Ginnie straightened her stance. "I knocked him down twice. I can't be too bad."

"You got lucky." Toran pointed an angry finger at her. "And you didn't do it alone."

Shrugging, she pushed the cat food container against the wall. "Fine, we're a good team then. You can't take Pierce on by yourself though. He'll hurt you."

Toran stiffened. "No, he won't. And if you stay out of it, he and I could settle it once and for all and *nobody* would get hurt."

"Oh, puh-lease." Ginnie rolled her eyes. "You might as well talk to a wall. Pierce's as thick as a brick."

"Kinda like you." Toran turned away from her.

"Hey!" His words stung. "What's that supposed to mean? At least I understand English. Pierce only understands fists."

"You're every bit as stubborn as Gertrude. Only it's okay for her—she's a *real* goat."

"What's going on?" Dad asked, appearing out of nowhere in his work clothes, grimacing as he glanced from one twin to the other.

"Nothing," both twins replied.

"It doesn't sound like 'nothing'. Toran, why are you calling your sister names?"

"I didn't call her a name. I said she was *as stubborn as* Gertrude." Toran turned his back on both of them.

Dad arched an eyebrow. "What's she being stubborn about?"

Ginnie met Toran's gaze and exchanged silent warnings.

Her brother kicked the straw bale in front of him. "I just want her to let me deal with Pierce when we see him again. He's going to be furious with her and I don't want her to get hurt."

"Sounds like a good plan, Gin." Dad nodded at her twin. "Let Toran deal with Pierce."

"And what if Pierce hits him?" Ginnie's hands flew to her hips.

"I'm not watching *anybody* beat up my brother."

"Why would Pierce hit him?" Dad hung his thumb on his pants pocket. "Toran's just suggesting you let *him* smooth this over. Pierce has had two days to think about you knocking him down. I've been a little concerned myself. I think Toran's plan is a good one. Let him work this out for you. He's your brother, it's allowed."

Toran smirked at her, toggling his head in satisfaction.

Ginnie scowled. "I can do it myself."

"That was your motto when you were two." Dad smiled, winding her braid through his fingers. "Let's find a new one, shall we?"

The amusement in Dad's voice was too much.

After glaring at her brother, she whirled toward her dad. "You're only taking his side 'cause you're both guys. If *Mama* were here, she'd tell Toran to be grateful he had a sister who could actually fight. *She'd* be happy I helped him."

Dad's jaw tightened as he leaned toward her. "Please don't put words in your mother's mouth." He lowered his voice. "I'm sure she'd try to look at this from both sides and try to come up with a solution that would help each of you—just like I am. Toran has a workable plan. Let's go with that."

"Let's not."

"Fine. Figure out a new plan while you milk Gertrude."

"No!"

Dad took a step toward her. "No?"

Ginnie swallowed. "I mean, no, sir. I don't want to milk Gertrude. I'll go with Toran's plan, but ..." She planted her hands on her hips again. "You're *not* being fair."

Gertrude was an okay goat for everybody but Ginnie and Uncle Jake. She didn't like either of them and for whatever reason had a habit of stepping on their feet or knocking over the milk pail. Both Ginnie and her uncle avoided milking Gertrude whenever they could.

"Life isn't fair. But if you go with Toran's plan, I'll milk Gertrude. Just to show you I can be reasonable."

"Whatever." Resisting the urge to roll her eyes, Ginnie turned from him. "I have to take care of Calliope." She walked toward the front of the barn at normal speed. Just as she rounded the corner, she glanced back and saw Dad give a "thumbs up" to Toran.

Fury boiled.

She bolted out of the barn.

CHAPTER TWENTY-FIVE:
RIDING BAREBACK

C ome on, Calliope." Ginnie clicked her tongue and led her mare to the wrought iron chairs by the side of the farmhouse so she could mount her.

"Aren't you forgetting something?" Uncle Jake asked, coming out the side porch door.

Ginnie shook her head and jumped on Calliope's back.

"Does your Dad know you're riding bareback?"

"I just need to ride." Ginnie turned Calliope. "See ya."

"Whoa." Uncle Jake grabbed the halter. "It's safer with a saddle. Use it."

She blew out an impatient breath. "That would mean seeing Daddy again and I'm not talking to him."

Uncle Jake chuckled. "That does complicate things, but being the good uncle that I am, I can't in good conscience allow you to ride bareback, knowing your dad prefers you riding with a saddle. Why are you mad at my brother?"

"Because he's nuts. And so is *my* brother. Please let go, I'll be fine."

Uncle Jake smiled and shook his head. "Can you define 'nuts' for me?"

"Crazy. Loony. Nutburgers. Now please let go."

"Sorry, I need more information than that."

"Uncle Jake!"

"Fill in the blank." He handed her Calliope's reins. "I am risking getting grounded by riding bareback because …"

Ginnie didn't hesitate, fury mounting. "Because my dad is as pigheaded as my brother. They would rather see Toran beat up by Pierce than have me help him. They *actually* think Pierce is gonna listen to Toran tell him to back off." Ginnie recalled Pierce's angry, purple face when he found himself on the theater floor earlier and shook her head. "Pierce isn't the chatting type."

"Hmm." Uncle Jake ran his hand down Calliope's satiny neck. "Well, Toran can be pretty persuasive when he needs to be. He doesn't get riled easily. It could work."

"Not you, too."

"Trouble." He locked his eyes on hers. "While I admire your protectiveness *and* your feistiness, your way got you suspended and in trouble with your dad. It seems only fair that Toran should get a chance to try things *his* way."

A quick recollection of Pierce's balled fists made Ginnie shake her head. She glanced at her uncle. *Maybe I should tell him about the movies, then he'll know Toran won't have a chance.*

But even Uncle Jake's welcoming smile couldn't untie her tongue.

Pierce's not gonna tell people I knocked him down again. Uncle Jake'll just make me tell my dad and Daddy'll be mad. And I'm NOT painting that fence again.

Ginnie rubbed her aching arms and forced a smile to her lips. "Fine, but can *you* get my saddle? I really don't want to deal with Daddy right now."

"Sure. I'm heading that way. Come on."

Calliope kept pace with Uncle Jake all the way up the hill to the main barn. When Uncle Jake entered the barn for the saddle, Ginnie slid off Calliope.

Toran walked over to her. "Are you really going to let me deal with Pierce by myself?"

"Just until he threatens you."

"That's not the deal."

"Oh, yes it is."

"No, it's not." Toran waved a threatening hand and then shoved it in his front pocket.

"It is now."

"You leave Pierce *to me*. Dad said."

"Are you two still arguing about Pierce?" Dad appeared with Calliope's saddle, startling both twins. "We settled that. Toran will reason with him and you, Ginnie Maie, will let him."

"But ..."

"No buts." Dad handed Ginnie the saddle blanket and waited for her to adjust it before lifting the saddle onto Calliope's back. "Are you done with the chickens?"

"No."

"Do them before you ride Calliope."

"But ..." Ginnie gave a quick glance to Dad's tight jaw and sighed. "Yes, sir."

"Toran, please finish the hogs."

"Sure, Dad."

Ginnie adjusted and cinched the saddle, and then swung into it. "I'll put her in the pasture until I'm done with the chickens."

"Good thinking." Dad stroked Calliope's neck. "And Ginnie?"

"Yeah?"

"No bareback riding. You know better."

"I'm not." Ginnie turned from him when she felt her cheeks warm.

Uncle Jake ratted me out? I'm glad I didn't tell him about the movies.

Recalling Tillie's terrified face, she shuddered, tapped Calliope's sides, needing to get as much distance between herself and her family as she could.

CHAPTER TWENTY-SIX
AND THE DRAMA
CONTINUES...

After dinner, Toran dried the dishes that Ginnie washed. Ignoring Ginnie and responding to her with one word answers didn't discourage her from talking to him like Toran hoped it would.

"Seriously, Toran. You don't need to hold a grudge. You ought to be happy I didn't let Pierce hurt you ..." She glanced around and lowered her voice. "Or Tillie. We made a good team, why can't we talk to Pierce together?"

He let out a frustrated breath, trying to figure out how to get her to drop the subject. "Because I don't want a repeat of what happened the other day ..." It was his turn to look around and lower his voice. "Or today. I just want to fix this. Let me." He hated begging, but if it would get her to back off, he'd try anything.

"Pierce came after me today looking for a fight. He wasn't looking to talk."

Toran slapped the dish towel on the countertop. "Just because he's looking for a fight doesn't mean you have to give him one. Don't you get it? You embarrassed him. No guy wants to be beat up by a girl ... or protected by one."

"You didn't think I was wrong in first grade when I stopped that fourth grader from ruining your sugar cube igloo."

Of course she has to bring THAT up!

"It was a *teepee*, not an *igloo*."

Ginnie rolled her eyes. "Whatever. He made you cry and I made *him* cry. You told Dad we should have a 'hero party' for me like Pooh Bear had for Piglet when he helped Eeyore. You weren't mad at me then. You thought I was brave."

"We were six. Things change. Junior high's different." *How do I get her to shut up already?* "Dad says you have to let me deal with it. So drop it."

"Yeah, I love how the two of you ganged up on me." Ginnie held the sprayer like a gun while she rinsed a plate. "If Mama were here, she'd take *my* side."

"No, she wouldn't. She'd be on *my* side."

Ginnie snorted. "In your dreams. Daddy says she was a fearless trick rider. She wouldn't let some dumb boy threaten you. She'd probably embarrass you even more than I did by telling his mom. She might even threaten *his* mom."

"She just might," Buzz teased, as he and Dad entered the kitchen.

Ginnie grinned. "See?"

"Which would make this an even bigger mess than it needs to be." Dad frowned at Buzz and pointed a warning finger at Ginnie. "Stick to the plan. I'm tired of you two bickering about this."

"We were just talking. Can I go to Austin's? The dishes are just about done."

Dad nodded. "You two could use a little space. Maybe Austin can help you understand."

"Good luck with that." Toran muttered, rubbing at the plate harder. "She doesn't listen to anybody."

"Enough, Tor," Dad warned.

Ginnie swiveled toward Dad. "Austin thought I was *cool* to knock Pierce down. He's not afraid of a girl showing him up. I do it all the time."

"Some days I worry that you'll get too much attention from boys, but if you keep that up, maybe I don't need too." Dad winked at her, then opened the refrigerator door.

She rolled her eyes. "Any boy who thinks I need protecting better think again. I'm no sissy."

"Nobody's accusing you of being a sissy. But for your brother's sake, leave this alone."

Toran turned to his dad, frustrated. Having Dad championing him didn't feel much better than having Ginnie beat up Pierce for him.

"Why are you on *his* side?" Ginnie demanded.

"I'm not." Dad pulled out the jug of milk. "Finish up and ride with Austin. Feel free to leave Traxx in Calliope's dust and tell me all about it. Just change the record, okay?"

"She probably doesn't even know what a record is," Toran growled and shoved the plate he just dried in the cupboard, hating how petty he sounded.

Dad threw him a warning look when he turned around.

Toran swallowed. "Sorry. I'll finish up."

"Good idea. Ginnie go ahead." Dad narrowed his eyes. "I'll help Toran."

Terrific! She gets to go to Austin's and I get a lecture. What else can go wrong?

CHAPTER TWENTY-SEVEN: GINNIE GOES TO AUSTIN'S

B red for trick riding, roping, and barrel racing, Calliope cantered Ginnie quickly across the way to Austin's home, "Chandler's Crossing", two farms down.

Ginnie's spirits lifted when she caught sight of the apple orchard to her left and the grove of Christmas pine trees to her right. She liked how fall and winter resided in harmony, and the smell of pine wafted in the air, even though it was spring.

Dad had called Toran, Austin, and Ginnie "The Three Musketeers" for the longest time because they were always together. After Mama died, Austin's mom, Miss Lauren, cared for Ginnie and Toran when Uncle Ben and Vi couldn't, until they could go to school full time while Dad worked.

Chandler's Crossing was a second home to both Ginnie and Toran. Austin hurried over when she approached his two-story white panel board house.

Ginnie waved. "Do you want to ride together?"

"Sure, let me ask my mom. Meet me by the stable." Austin turned and ran into his house.

Ginnie rode Calliope over to the barn where Austin's black gelding, Traxx, stood. Ginnie dismounted and led Calliope to Traxx's water trough for a drink.

She waited for Austin to return. "My mom said yes."

"Cool, where do you want to ride?"

"Wherever."

They raced the horses around Austin's land. After Ginnie and Calliope beat Austin and Traxx three out of five times, Austin suggested they go over to the West farm.

Ginnie nodded her agreement. "Yeah, maybe Toran will get over being mad at me sooner if you come over."

"Why's he mad?"

"Because I flattened Pierce for him. *Again.*" Ginnie grinned. "We had a run-in at the movies this afternoon and Pierce came after us. I knocked him down … *twice.*"

Austin laughed. "Twice? Oh, man! Poor Toran!"

"Poor *Toran*? Don't you mean poor *Pierce*?" Ginnie glared at her friend. "*Toran* should be grateful. He'd be 'poor, *hurt* Toran' if I wasn't there. Stop taking his side."

Austin shrugged. "Well, no guy wants a girl beating up another guy for him. And *especially* not his little sister."

"I'm only five minutes younger." Ginnie perched her hands on her hips. "And I'm a better fighter."

"Still, you're a girl and his sister. His *twin* sister no less. It's not cool."

"Why should that matter?" Ginnie waved him away and mounted Calliope. "Never mind, don't come home with me, you're being as dumb as he is."

A stunned look crossed Austin's face. "Sorry. It was awesome how you flattened him at school. But it woulda been better for Toran if you had let *him* do it."

Ginnie shook her head in disgust. "Boys are so dumb."

"Hey, chill out. I still wanna ride with you." He mounted Traxx and made him even with Calliope. "I said I was sorry."

Ginnie rolled her eyes. "Fine. Just quit saying I was wrong to help my brother. *I wasn't.*"

Austin grinned. "Deal. 'Heart of the Wests', here we come." Austin took the lead.

Ginnie smiled and followed.

She loved the name of her family farm. Her great-great-great-great-great-great-great grandfather, Obadiah West, named their original homestead "Heart of the Wests" in commemoration of their trek west from New York.

He and his young bride loved the play on words of their family name. Obadiah insisted that Eloise West and their five sons, were the "heart" of their operation, and fashioned their cattle brand out of a "W" and a heart.

The brand stood as a sentinel, nestled in the middle of four silhouetted horses on the offset T-shaped signpost mounted at the entrance of their property.

They lined up with the sign.

"On your mark, get set, GO!"

Ginnie and Austin raced down the lane. Traxx and Calliope took turns leading the way.

Ginnie grinned as Calliope pulled firmly into the lead. Austin hunkered forward. They reached the three shade maples and slowed. "Yes!" Ginnie called out.

"Aw, man. Almost!" Austin shrugged and turned Traxx toward the hay barn on the left.

Ginnie followed, catching movement ahead of her, near the family's row of parked cars. She couldn't place one of the cars. She scanned the bodies congregating behind the vehicles. Panic gripped her belly, pulsing a shudder over her entire body.

Dad, Uncle Jake, Toran, and Buzz faced Pierce and his father, who stood arguing with Dad and Toran. She pulled the reins to stop Calliope. "Whoa, girl."

This can't be good.

CHAPTER TWENTY-EIGHT:
THE OWENS'
ACCUSATION

D ad and the others stood in front of the family's parked cars. "Ginnie, please tell us what happened at the movies." He nodded at Pierce and his father.

The aggravated look in Dad's eyes had as much intensity as the electric bug zapper hanging from the woodshed to her left. Ginnie got the feeling if she didn't say the right thing, *she* might get squished like a bug.

After running her hand down Calliope's neck in an effort to comfort herself as much as her horse, Ginnie turned toward Pierce. He sported a swollen black eye that was turning slightly green and dark purple. *Wow. Toran must have hit him harder than I thought. There's no way I'd believe that shiner was going to appear.*

She glanced at Toran. "There's not much to tell."

"Try." Dad's one word answer spoke volumes.

She explained the popcorn flying, Tillie being upset, Pierce's tight hold, the punch, and Toran's knee popping up in Pierce's face, finishing with, "It wasn't a big deal."

Mr. Owens pointed to Pierce's eye. "That doesn't seem like a big deal to you, young lady?"

Dad took a step closer to Mr. Owens, putting himself between the burly man and Calliope.

Ginnie shrugged. "I don't know how that happened. It didn't seem like Toran hit him very hard at the time--but Pierce started it."

Her eyes narrowed, matching Mr. Owens'.

Mr. Owens' face puckered as he pointed at Pierce. "Are you going to let her blame *you*, boy?"

Pierce ducked his head, taking a quick step backward.

For a moment, Ginnie was sure she saw the aggressive lines of his face slump into defeat, before his scowl deepened again. "No way! She's lying!"

She glanced at Toran, but her brother's eyes were glued on Austin. Ginnie swallowed and sat up straighter. "The man behind me broke it up before Pierce could hit me back. All's I did was protect Tillie— Pierce dared me to, so I knocked him on his rear, Mr. Owens." Ginnie glared at Pierce and repeated for her dad's benefit. "He told me to."

Mr. Owens turned to Pierce. "You let the same girl toss you *twice? That can't be right!*"

Ginnie winced at his ugly tone.

Buzz stepped next to Dad, in front of Calliope. "Their stories are the same." His voice bore no malice, reminding Ginnie of Uncle Ben. Buzz truly was his father's son, quiet and full of self-control. Uncle Jake moved next to Buzz, standing as sentries in front of Calliope with her dad.

"Because they're twins!" Pierce kicked the dirt. "Of course they'll tell the same story!"

"Being twins doesn't make us liars!" Toran protested, taking a step forward while pointing at Pierce. "You shouldn't have grabbed Tillie!"

Dad moved in front of Toran and motioned for him to back up. Toran's glare stayed fixed on Pierce a moment before he moved.

"Three against one is still wrong!" Mr. Owens proclaimed, glowering at Ginnie.

His false accusation set Ginnie's mouth in gear. "That's *not* what happened. Pierce started it. He grabbed Tillie and dared me to make him let go!"

Mr. Owen's intimidating sneer made her pause.

Uncle Jake's jaw set tight as he took hold of Calliope's bridle and clicked at her. Calliope backed up a couple of steps. Ginnie felt safe enough to finish her side of the story. "And then he pushed Toran before we did anything to him. Are we supposed to let him hurt us?"

"*Of course not.*" Uncle Jake squared his body to Mr. Owens, his tone dripping with warning. "Ginnie can obviously hold her own. *Your* kid ought to quit while he's behind."

Mr. Owens balled his fist. "Wanna repeat that?"

"Any time." Uncle Jake moved forward, raising his own fist. "I'm *not* a little girl and I'll drop you like a sack of oats."

Ginnie and Toran exchanged open mouths. *Go, Uncle Jake!*

Dad stepped between the two hotheads. "Jake, stop it! We're trying to *avoid* a fight. Back up. This isn't solving anything." He turned to Mr. Owens. "Ray, I asked you to come over so my kids can apologize to Pierce and help them all come to an understanding. If we can't resolve this tonight, then let's just agree to keep them apart. If they see each other at school, they can simply turn and walk away. We never have to have this conversation again."

Mr. Owens muttered something inaudible.

Ginnie's jaw dropped. *Dad asked them over?* He threw Ginnie a no-nonsense look.

I guess I better apologize. She took a breath. "I'm sorry about our misunderstanding, Pierce."

Pierce's eyes narrowed, even the multi-colored one. His cheeks flamed.

Mr. Owens thumped Pierce on the back hard enough to cause him to stumble.

Calliope shied.

Pierce righted himself quickly, his T-shirt sleeve pulling up to reveal an old bruise.

"Whoa, girl!" Ginnie soothed, grimacing at Pierce.

"What do you need to say, *boy*?" Mr. Owens snapped.

"Sorry!" Pierce hissed, his look promising this would be continued at a later time.

Dad cleared his throat. "Toran?"

"Sorry, Pierce. I didn't mean to black your eye." Toran sucked in his cheeks, but not before Ginnie saw the slight smile on his lips. Judging by the ugly look Pierce sent Toran, he hadn't missed Toran's amusement either.

Austin let out a chortle and turned from them.

Dad pushed Uncle Jake lightly to back him up even more. "All right then, let's call it a night. I had hoped this would be completely resolved, but maybe calling a truce will have to be good enough for now."

That's probably not gonna happen.

He reached a hand to Pierce's shoulder. "I am sorry for my kids' part in this and we'll be having a little chat about what happened." Dad glanced between Toran and Ginnie, and narrowed his eyes in warning. "Maybe in a few days—when we've all had some time to cool down—we can settle this once and for all. But until then, I'll have them keep their distance. Can I count on you to do the same?"

Pierce offered a begrudging nod, ducking his head when his dad barked his name. Mr. Owens continued to chew on Pierce something awful, mostly about being a wimp, as they walked to their car. Ginnie almost felt sorry for him— until they slammed their doors—startling both horses.

Dad stepped forward, took hold of each of the reins and calmed the two horses. "Austin, I think it would be best if you went home." Dad pointed down the lane. "Buzz, please put Calliope up. Virginia and Victor, go to your rooms!"

He handed Calliope's reins to Buzz.

Ginnie started to protest, but took one look at Dad and closed her mouth. Keeping her dad happy may not be the best reason to do something, but when he looked like *that*, she knew better than to cross him.

Austin shrugged at her and turned Traxx down the lane. "Maybe tomorrow?"

"I hope so." Ginnie slid out of the saddle, avoided her dad the best she could, and followed Toran up the front porch stairs, swallowing hard.

CHAPTER TWENTY-NINE:
THE FALLOUT

V irginia Maie, come here."

Ginnie hurried to Toran's room, where Dad stood with his arms folded across his chest, glancing from one to the other of them. She'd been hoping Uncle Jake would calm him down before he came upstairs to talk to them, but he still looked pretty ticked off.

"Sit!" Dad pointed at Toran's bed.

Ginnie hurried to obey, exchanging a glance of 'Yikes!' with her brother. Toran paled.

"Refresh my memory, Virginia Maie Stratton West, *the second*. Did you, or did you *not*, get suspended from school three days ago?"

Ginnie cringed at the use of her full name. That was never a good sign. "Yes, sir, I did."

"*For what?*"

Wincing, she looked beyond his scowl to the model airplanes hanging from the ceiling. She counted five of them before she gave Dad her full attention. "For fighting."

"And the fact that you just spent *two* days painting almost a quarter-mile of fence because you got suspended had no impact on you. *Why?*" Dad waved in the general direction of their lane and gave her no time to reply. "Because I was foolish enough to think you're twelve now and I should be able to reason with you?"

Ginnie's stomach lurched as she recalled Tillie's face and how her friend froze, terrified, when Pierce grabbed her arm. She threw a pleading look at Dad, not being able to put her thoughts into words.

Dad drummed his fingers on his belt buckle.

Ginnie gulped. "You weren't there. He grabbed Tillie. She turned white—like a ghost. I didn't think about fighting, only about helping her. I wanted him to let go of her so she wouldn't be afraid anymore." She looked Dad square in the eye. "That's the truth."

He spun toward Toran. "And you?"

"I tried to stop it. I didn't want either of them hurt."

"Hmmm!" Dad paced back and forth, twice. "So … when were you planning to tell me about your little run-in with Pierce today?"

Each shrugged.

"Well?" His fingers drummed louder. "Virginia Maie?"

He was definitely angrier with her than Toran. Four 'Virginias' in five minutes and two with her middle name meant she was in big trouble. It wouldn't surprise her if she'd be painting the fence blue after all. She turned to Toran for help.

He swallowed big and shrugged again.

He's useless. Where's Uncle Jake when I need him? "Well …" Ginnie stalled, not wanting to tell him the whole truth. "We didn't think it was a big deal, so we decided not to tell you at all. Nobody got hurt."

He shook his head hard enough to make his curls sway. "Except Pierce--did you see his eye?" Dad whirled away, his stern tone cracking. Ginnie thought she heard a note of humor in Dad's voice. He forced a cough. *Maybe he's not so mad about the black eye, but he's hot about us not telling him about the fight.*

Toran and Ginnie exchanged tentative smiles and then whipped them off their faces when Dad's waves swayed again. His eyes darted back and forth between them.

Toran stood. "Pierce started it both times. He dared Ginnie to help Tillie. *And* he pushed me before any of us touched him. *Honest!*"

Ginnie jumped to her feet. "I bet Pierce only brought it up because of his eye. We got the better of him twice, but *only* after he started it. *Honest!*"

"Sit!" Dad barked, pointing at the bed.

Toran sat, followed by Ginnie. "The guy that held him away, even *he* said it was Pierce's fault."

Dad let his gaze rest on each of them. "I've heard enough. You're both grounded for two days and don't say a word Virginia Maie or I'll make it five!"

Ginnie clamped her mouth shut.

"Why are *we* in trouble?" Toran complained, holding both palms up. "Pierce was picking on *us*."

"Because you didn't tell me when you got home and I had to find out about it from the likes of Ray Owens. You shouldn't have hid this from me." Dad pointed to Ginnie. "Not a word!"

Ginnie turned, harrumphing. Toran's neat desk made her madder. She clenched her fists.

"Can we talk about this?" Toran asked.

Dad looked him square in the eye. "*Not ... right ... now*. Get ready for bed, both of you!"

"Yes, sir," Toran quickly replied.

"Virginia Maie?"

"You said not to say a word. So I didn't."

"You know 'yes, sir' and 'no, sir' are allowed," Dad scolded. "*You* are now grounded for *three* days—for being a smart aleck."

"That's not fair."

Dad drew himself up to his fullest height. "Would you like to try for a week?"

Too angry to be intimidated, Ginnie snapped, "*No*, sir!"

"Watch your tone. Get ready for bed, and brush your teeth. I'll be back in a few minutes when I've calmed down." He wagged a warning finger at her, then turned on his cowboy heels and left.

As soon as she heard his boots hit the runner on the wooden stairs, Ginnie jerked her head toward Toran.

"What was that about? Why's he picking on *me*?"

Toran shrugged. "I don't know. You heard him though—get ready for bed."

Ginnie stormed to her room. She opened her drawers to find her pajamas and slammed them closed. Changing for bed, she thought of Austin and remembered they were supposed to be riding. She stomped to the bathroom, scrubbed her teeth, and went back to her room. Her clock read 6:45.

And we have to go to bed? Pathetic! I wish Uncle Jake was our dad. He'd take us out for ice cream to celebrate instead of grounding us for defending ourselves! She giggled at the thought. Toran appeared in her doorway. "What's so funny?"

Ginnie grinned and repeated her thoughts.

Toran smiled.

Ginnie froze.

A shiver ran through her when Dad appeared behind her twin.

CHAPTER THIRTY:
YIKES!

Sugar beets! How am I gonna get out of this?

Ginnie peeked at Dad as a sick feeling washed over her.

A hurt look crossed his face before his eyes narrowed in anger. Toran turned slowly to face their dad.

"You are *not* being grounded for defending yourselves. You *are* being grounded for not being honest with me." He placed a hand on his hip. "You might want to remember I consider it my business to know when my kids get into fights. I also *expect* my kids to tell me before anyone else does, got it?"

His tone left no doubt as to the answer he expected.

"Yes, sir," Ginnie and Toran chorused quickly.

She felt Dad's stare.

"You think Jake would make a better dad?" He turned from her before she could make eye contact with him.

"Maybe tonight he would," Ginnie sulked. She took note of Toran's meticulously neat bookshelves, each book arranged perfectly by size. *Boy, is my brother a neat freak.*

"Hmmm." Dad turned to Toran. "How about you?"

"I have no comment on the subject." His voice was very matter of fact—neat and sensible—like the stacking of his books.

Dad turned to Ginnie. "So how do you think Jake would handle your bullheadedness and penchant for pushing the limits?"

Ginnie took a step back from him. "Do you want me to be honest?"

"No, lie to me. Because that's how I've raised you."

His sarcasm wasn't very reassuring. "Are you asking as my dad or as my fun uncle?"

"Is that how you see Jake--as the fun uncle who does whatever he wants and I'm the bear who makes you behave?" His fingers danced on his belt buckle again, which she realized sported a 3-D image of a pewter grizzly bear. Not a happy coincidence. But at least the buckle bear didn't look as angry as her dad did.

Pretty sure from his tone that he didn't want her honest answer, Ginnie racked her brain for a reply that wouldn't turn three days of grounding into two weeks.

"You started this line of thought. Answer me ... *honestly.*"

Ginnie glanced at Toran, who shook his head at her, warning her not to humor their dad.

"What Uncle Jake would do if he was my dad or do I see you as a bear?" *How am I going to answer him without catching more trouble? Good going, Gin!*

"Both."

That was too quick. "Do you promise not to ground me longer if I'm honest with you?"

"Yes."

"What about extra chores?" Ginnie smiled a little as she stalled.

"No extra chores either."

"No docking my allowance?"

His smile flipped upside down. "You're trying my patience again."

Ginnie beamed him her brightest grin. "Okay then. Yes. I think you're a bear—a grizzly bear when I mess up and a teddy bear when I don't."

He chuckled. "Nice save. And how would Jake handle your bullheadedness?"

"I don't think he'd be upset because he doesn't worry about things like you do."

"Are you saying that I should lighten up?"

Well, yes! Duh. She toned down her smile and gave a slight nod. "A *little* wouldn't hurt."

"I'll take it under consideration." He raised his eyebrows. "Anything else?"

Ginnie shook her head and wrapped her arms around his waist. "Nope. I'm glad *you're* my dad."

"You're just saying that so I reduce your grounding."

"No, it's the truth. But if you want to unground us, I'm okay with that." She tried to keep a straight face, knowing he might change his mind.

He looked at each of them. "Tell you what. I'll reduce both of your groundings to *just* tomorrow if I only hear 'Yes, sir, I'll be happy too,' whenever I ask you to do something. Deal?"

Ginnie peeked at Toran, who replied. "Honest?"

Dad nodded. "Cross my heart."

"It's a deal!" Toran agreed as Ginnie nodded.

Dad kissed the top of each child's head. "Goodnight, guys."

"Night, Dad," they replied together and headed for their own beds.

Just as Ginnie started to doze, a tremor ran through her. She sat upright.

That was too easy! Daddy never ungrounds us. What's the catch? Her thoughts tumbled wildly. *Hmmm. What would he consider a proper punishment for sneaking?*

Certain he would come up with something worse than painting the fence, Ginnie groaned as she punched her pillows. Then she remembered that he was raised by Uncle Ben, who had a knack for making a point without coming off too fearsome, but making her extremely miserable just the same.

Moaning, she dropped onto her pillow. "We're toast! And not just regular toast, we're *burnt* toast!"

☐

CHAPTER THIRTY-ONE:
A VERY BAD DAY

T he next morning, Toran and Austin followed Ginnie and Tillie off the school bus, then moved in front of them.

Toran stopped in front of her so quickly, Ginnie nearly ran him over. "Gin, Pierce's watching us and he's furious. Don't mess with him." Toran nodded toward the front of their school. "Let's go through the library. Dad said to avoid him, plus, we're already grounded."

Ginnie peeked around him to check out Pierce. His eye looked even worse than it did last night. He wore a long sleeve green t-shirt pushed nearly to his elbows.

The humidity's bad already. He's gonna be hot today.

Ginnie felt Pierce's gaze even as they turned from him to go to the library.

"Wow, he's ticked!" Austin glanced over his shoulder at Pierce, not even trying to be discreet. He winked at Ginnie. "You probably ought to avoid him 'til he cools off. He's not going to let you drop him a third time."

She didn't miss his amused tone. "Ya think?"

"It's not funny, Ginnie. He's scary mad," Tillie said, her voice quivering.

Toran touched Tillie's elbow. "It's okay."

"I don't think Pierce agrees. You said he was pretty mad last night when he came to the farm. He's had plenty of time 'to stew' as Uncle Ben would say."

"Lighten up, Tillie. He started it." Ginnie rolled her eyes. "He'll chill out."

Toran threw Ginnie an exasperated look. "Not if you goad him. Leave him alone."

"Goad? Talk like a real person, will ya?" Ginnie shook her head at him.

"Goad means tease. You just keep your distance. Dad's only going to forgive us this one grounding. You fight with Pierce again and you're going to be painting the fence blue and then green, and then something else. *And* he'll ground us 'til we're in high school."

"I know what it means. You *just think* you're so smart." Ginnie turned from him.

Tillie frowned. "He's right, Gin. And there's no stranger to help. Mr. Reed already suspended you for two days. It'll probably be for a week next time."

"You're a worrywart. And Toran's over-anxious. Get a grip, both of you." A smile buzzed Ginnie's lips. "Pierce's dad was even madder than Daddy. I think he has more to worry about than us."

Austin opened the library door and waited for the girls to walk through. Tillie grimaced. "His dad isn't very nice. Remember when he had to bring Pierce's science project in fourth grade and he yelled at him because Pierce forgot part of it at home? He was scary."

"I remember Pierce grabbing you last night and scaring *you*." Ginnie looked to Toran and Austin for help, then locked her gaze on Tillie. "He deserved to be yelled at."

Toran shook his head. "His dad was really mad. Pierce probably got in a lot more trouble than us."

Austin gave her a half-smile.

Ginnie recalled Tillie's pale face and allowed no sympathetic words to cross her lips. "He should. He lied and *he* started it. He shouldn't have grabbed Tillie."

The warning bell rang.

Toran latched his eyes on her. "Stay clear of him. He'll try to pound you for sure. Shooting your mouth off at him isn't going to make things better."

Ginnie flipped her braids from one shoulder to the other. "Yeah, yeah, yeah."

Toran grabbed her upper arm and held tight. "I mean it, Virginia. Leave him alone."

Fury coursed through her. "Let go, *Victor*."

"Give me your word you'll stay away from him."

Ginnie tilted her head. "No, and you better let go before I knock *you* on your rear." She tried to pull her arm from Toran's hold.

Toran gripped harder. "After you promise."

Time seemed to stop as they glared at each other. Ginnie repeated her threat telepathically while Toran held tight. Ginnie considered her options. Just as she decided she would force him to let go, Austin tapped Toran's arm. "We're gonna be late."

Toran's eyes stayed steeled on hers, even as his grip loosened. His silent warning found its target.

Ginnie realized just in time this wasn't just about Pierce. Her brother had a point to make.

Tillie tugged at Ginnie's hand, pulling her away from Toran. "Austin's right—we need to go."

The tremble in Tillie's voice startled Ginnie. "Fine."

She threw Toran a look promising to finish this later and followed Tillie to the hallway.

They broke into a jog and hurried to their classroom.

CHAPTER THIRTY-TWO:
LUNCH WITH
MRS. JOHNSON

Ginnie stewed all through English class and half of math, thinking about Toran's unspoken challenge, and mulling all the possible outcomes. She and Toran rarely argued, let alone fought. It just wasn't allowed.

She remembered the last time they had a physical confrontation, just before their eighth birthday. Ginnie was so mad she threw a stuffed animal at him. It missed Toran, but knocked out the first model airplane he had ever built.

It took only long enough for him to see it crash to the ground before he pushed Ginnie down. She got up and rushed at him, determined to return the favor.

Uncle Jake pulled them apart a couple minutes later. Dad walked in and took over lecturing them. Then he grounded them for the first time ever, making them work side by side for the next two days through what felt like a million chores. It didn't take long to figure out that hitting each other wasn't worth the punishment.

Ginnie wondered how far Toran would have gone if she had continued to resist.

"Ginnie, pay attention," Mrs. Johnson scolded. Her teacher stood directly in front of her desk. "Please tell the class the answer to number six."

Ginnie looked to Tillie for a clue.

Mrs. Johnson stepped into her line of vision and tapped Ginnie's textbook. "Here's where you'll find the answer."

Her cheeks heated.

Mrs. Johnson took a closer look at Ginnie's paper. Only two problems were solved. Mrs. Johnson frowned. "You may see me at lunch to catch up. Do problem seven now. Andrew, what's the answer to number six?"

Ginnie couldn't concentrate as she worked the problem. Her anger grew as she thought of Toran's ability to do math problems in his head. Dad expected straight 'A's from both, but schoolwork came easier to Toran.

"Ginnie, number seven please."

She struggled to keep her voice even. "Three."

Mrs. Johnson paused. "Close. The answer is negative three. Watch the negative signs, please."

"Yes'm."

Some of her classmates laughed. Ginnie refused to look in Tillie's direction, even though she knew she would find sympathy. When Mrs. Johnson released the class, Ginnie took her time getting her lunch sack.

"I'll ask if I can eat with you," Tillie offered.

"That won't be necessary, Tillie. Ginnie will be having lunch with me today," Mrs. Johnson replied as she approached the girls. Her tone was surprisingly inviting.

Tillie threw Ginnie a sympathetic smile just before she turned and left.

"Ginnie, please come sit at my desk." Mrs. Johnson pulled a chair next to hers. Mrs. Johnson held out a peanut butter cookie.

Ginnie looked at her teacher, puzzled.

"You're having a rough week. Do you want to talk about it?"

Ginnie stared into Mrs. Johnson's kind eyes and shrugged. "There's nothing to talk about."

Mrs. Johnson smiled. "If that's true, why did I notice you muttering to yourself quite a bit this morning?"

Ginnie shrugged again, feeling heat rise along her neck. "Pierce Owens came over last night and lied about something that happened."

A concerned look crossed Mrs. Johnson's face.

Ginnie bit into the cookie. It wasn't as good as Vi's peanut butter cookies, but still tasty.

"Did you have something to do with his black eye?"

"No. Toran caught him with his knee after Pierce grabbed Tillie. He just wanted Pierce to let her go."

Mrs. Johnson drew in a sharp breath. "I saw his eye. It looks terrible."

Ginnie's gaze dropped to her teacher's desk.

"What did Pierce lie about?"

"Us ganging up on him. He came after me, and when Tillie tried to help me, he hurt her."

"Why do you think he did that?"

"Because he's a bully."

"Why do you think Pierce bullies other kids?"

Ginnie shrugged.

"Do you think if he had a good friend like you have in Tillie—and Tillie has in you—that he'd still want to bully other kids?"

"I don't know. But he better not touch Tillie again."

Mrs. Johnson laid her hand on Ginnie's. "Would you be willing to try an experiment for me?"

Ginnie shrugged again. "Doing what?"

"To see if you can gather more flies with honey than vinegar."

"Why would I want flies?"

Mrs. Johnson smiled. "Not real flies. I hear how angry you are about Pierce hurting Tillie. But what's going to happen if you tell *him* how angry you are?"

Ginnie took a second to think before she replied. "We'll probably get into another fight."

"Probably." Mrs. Johnson agreed. "Then what'll happen?"

"Mr. Reed will suspend me again."

"And I bet your dad won't be happy about that."

Ginnie shook her head in agreement. "He won't."

"So maybe instead of arguing with Pierce, you can think of something to say to him that won't lead to another fight?"

"My dad invited him to our house last night to work things out."

"How did that go?"

"Not so good. My uncle threatened to punch his dad and his dad wasn't real happy about it."

Mrs. Johnson's eyes widened. "What if I had you and Pierce work on a special project together in my room, or with Mrs. Danielson, the school counselor? We could do something fun, like draw posters for the end-of-the-year carnival. I could even bring ice cream sandwiches."

"I doubt Pierce would agree to it."

"I'd like to ask him anyway. Maybe Toran, Tillie, Levi, Steve, Tuck, and Austin could come as well. Would you be willing to try?"

It took every ounce of self-control Ginnie had to not roll her eyes. "Pierce is a jerk."

"Maybe he *acts* like a jerk because he doesn't know how to be a friend." Mrs. Johnson gently squeezed her hand. "The other students like you, Ginnie. If you and your friends were nice to Pierce, then other kids might be as well. At least think about it, okay?"

"Okay, but you're asking for a miracle."

Her teacher smiled. "It's a good thing I believe in miracles then, isn't it? Finish your lunch and I'll help you with your math.

CHAPTER THIRTY-THREE:
AND THE DAY
GETS WORSE

During social studies, Tillie and Ginnie were called to Mr. Reed's office.

"What do you think the principal wants us for?" Tillie asked, her voice anxious.

Ginnie pushed aside her own fears and forced a smile. "I didn't fight with anyone, so it can't be too bad." They were surprised to see Toran pacing in the waiting room.

"What did you do *now?*" he demanded of Ginnie as they approached.

"You're here too. What did *you* do?"

"Nothing." He returned her glare and then searched Tillie's face. "Don't worry."

Oh sure. Be nice to Tillie. She's not your sister, at least not yet. The change in his tone brought back Ginnie's frustration with him.

Before she could say anything else, Mr. Reed appeared from behind Mrs. Stewart's desk. "Good. You're all here. Please come into my office." He motioned toward his door.

Toran threw her a warning look, reminding Ginnie of their dad, then smiled at Tillie.

Just what I need, another Dad. I'd rather have Mama.

Her grimace brought a shake of Mr. Reed's head.

Lovely. I haven't done anything wrong and he thinks I'M the troublemaker. Just lovely.

Someone had added a chair since her visit to his office on Monday. "Please sit."

Each of them sat, with Tillie in the middle.

Mr. Reed's glance took them in, one by one. Tillie paled and twirled a lock of her long brown hair around her finger, the way she always did when she was worried.

Ginnie and Toran exchanged concerned looks.

Toran set his jaw and asked, "Are we in trouble?"

Mr. Reed leaned forward, his brown eyes meeting Toran's surprised gaze. "Yes and no. I'd appreciate it if you'd tell me what happened at the movies yesterday."

Toran looked from Tillie to Ginnie, prompting her to protest. "I didn't say a word."

Mr. Reed cleared his throat. "I just want to get to the bottom of Pierce's black eye. He says you three jumped him."

Toran, Ginnie and Tillie exchanged surprised, irritated, and horrified looks in turn.

Ginnie sprang to her feet. "He's lying. And besides, *he* started it."

Mr. Reed pointed his finger at Ginnie and then tapped it downwards. He waited for her to sit.

Tillie's face paled even more as Toran found his voice. "Pierce approached *us*."

"I'm not accusing anybody of anything, I just want clarification," Mr. Reed said.

Ginnie's mouth went into overdrive as she explained what happened. On occasion, Toran inserted a few words, but Tillie only nodded her agreement.

When they finished, Mr. Reed nodded. "That's a different story than what Pierce told. Normally, I would interview you separately, but I am rushed today. I am going to request that you stay away from him. He isn't in any of your classes for the rest of the day, so I expect that not to be a problem. Do we have an understanding?" Mr. Reed's eyes held Ginnie's a bit longer than Toran's or Tillie's.

"Yes, sir." Irritation graced Ginnie's reply.

Mr. Reed's eyebrows arched.

Tillie and Toran chorused, "Yes, sir."

Mr. Reed focused on Tillie. "I know I can count on you to stay away from him. Mr. West, I expect *you* to help your sister see the benefit of obedience in this situation. A second suspension won't look good on her transcript."

The fact that he knew Toran thought about things like that both annoyed and surprised Ginnie.

"Yes, sir." Toran shot a glance at Ginnie that suggested she respond to the principal as well.

Ginnie nodded. "Yes, sir."

Mr. Reed chuckled and stood. "It's nice to hear the occasional 'yes, sir.' I used it often growing up, speaking with your great-uncle especially. He always had a way with young people."

Ginnie and Toran exchanged shrugs and looked expectantly at Mr. Reed.

He motioned to his door. "Miss West?"

"Yes, Mr. Reed?"

"Please make sure if I need to see you again, it isn't Pierce-related. Win a reading award or something, okay?" The amusement in his voice reminded her of Uncle Jake. She could picture the two of them being friends better. Uncle Jake was quite a tease.

Toran snorted, then had the decency to look embarrassed when Mr. Reed raised an eyebrow.

The color returned to Tillie's cheeks when she giggled.

Ginnie clamped her jaw shut before she could respond sarcastically. *Wow, I must be channeling Daddy.* Her self-control only lasted until they entered the hallway. She leveled Toran with a glare. "That was just s-o-o-o funny."

He laughed. "Actually it was. *You?* Winning a reading award? *Puh-lease.*"

Tillie hugged Ginnie. "Toran, be nice. She could."

"Not in this lifetime."

"You know, Victor Alexander West, Mr. Reed only said to stay away from *Pierce.* He didn't say anything about not flattening *you.*" Ginnie enjoyed his double-take while he processed her threat.

"In your dreams." Toran waved her off and turned to Tillie. "What's your next class?"

Ginnie grabbed Tillie's hand. "Same as mine—social studies." For once she was glad Toran wasn't in her class. She liked being with her brother most of the time, but his attitude the last couple days was "dancing on her last nerve," as Uncle Ben had a habit of saying.

Her twin smirked. "See you after school."

"Yeah, yeah, yeah."

CHAPTER THIRTY-FOUR:
THE THREAT

After the last bell rang, Ginnie and Tillie headed to their bus. "Oh, snap," Ginnie muttered.

"What?"

"I forgot my math book."

"Hurry and get it. I'll let the bus driver know."

"Thanks." Ginnie turned back to the school and ran to the door. As she rushed through it, she felt a tug on her wrist. It stopped her in her tracks.

Pierce Owens gripped her wrist in his hand. "We have something to finish."

Ginnie studied his face while her dad's, Mrs. Johnson's, and Mr. Reed's warnings tumbled in her head. She tried to pull away. A shiver of panic surged through her when her wrist didn't come free of Pierce's grasp.

Finally, her brain connected to her mouth. "Not here we don't. I'm not getting suspended over you again."

Pierce's eyes narrowed. "Fine." The one word held a multitude of tones, all malicious. "Soon."

He twisted her wrist until she had to clench her teeth to not cry out, and then released her, disappearing out the door into a sea of students.

CHAPTER THIRTY-FIVE:
RIDING HOME

You're not saying much and you're barely listening," Tillie complained while shaking Ginnie's arm. "What's wrong?"

Ginnie stared out the bus window, watching the houses and trees rush by, feeling sick to her stomach. She rubbed at the wrist Pierce twisted, the slight burn gone from her wrist but not from her mind.

The bus slowed, blasting air brakes loudly in her ears.

"Tell me what's wrong," Tillie demanded.

Her impatient tone caused Ginnie to turn from the window. "Nothing. I was just thinking."

Someone got off the bus and it started moving again.

"Virginia West, you're lying and you'd best stop. I hate it when you're grounded." Tillie's outrage tossed the image of Pierce's bruised and threatening face out of her mind.

"Get a grip, Tillie. I haven't done anything wrong."

"But you will. I *know* you. Whatever's on your mind is going to lead to trouble." Tillie's lips formed a pout. "And we had plans this weekend, *remember?*"

"Fine. I got it." She smiled at her friend. "You worry too much."

"And you don't worry enough."

Ginnie rolled her eyes. "Yes, Mom."

Tillie offered a relieved giggle.

Ginnie considered Mrs. Johnson's advice to be friends with Pierce. She glanced at her wrist and scowled.

Not likely.

"Come on, Gin, it's our stop." Toran's words took a second for her to comprehend.

Ginnie waited for Tillie to leave their seat, snatched at her backpack, and followed them off the bus. When the bus began moving, Toran stood in front of her. She nearly walked into him. "Stop doing that, Tor!"

"What's going on?" This time concern graced his tone.

Her defenses melted and she told him about her run-in with Pierce, trying to ignore the betrayed look on Tillie's face. "What do I do?"

"I don't know, but at least he's agreed not to fight you at school. Maybe I can talk to him."

"I'm not afraid of him, Toran," Ginnie snapped.

"You should be." He reached for her wrist. "It's still pink."

"Because I've been rubbing it."

He dropped her hand. "Ginnie, you're in over your head." Toran blew out a frustrated breath, then caught a shake of Tillie's head. "We can fix this … together, but you've got to give me some time to think it through."

Toran nodded at the newly-painted fence. "Remember what happens when you're impulsive?"

Ginnie's frustration rose.

"Hey, don't get mad. Promise me you'll give me time to get a plan together and then we'll deal with Pierce, *together*, all right?"

Tillie's sympathetic nod chilled Ginnie's desire to fight. "Listen to him. He's just trying to help."

Not having a better plan at the moment, Ginnie nodded, hoping Tillie's faith in her twin was well placed.

Toran adjusted his backpack and lowered his voice. "I'm sorry for what happened between us at school today. I'm still a little ticked about you decking Pierce after I asked you to leave him to me."

"I'm not helpless, Toran—"

"I never said you were, but you promised you'd give me a little time to try something else." He smiled at her, disarming her anger. "You can always fight him again if my way doesn't work out. I'm sure Dad will be happy to buy that blue paint."

Ginnie rolled her eyes, allowing him to lighten her mood, realizing they were on the same side. The three of them walked together the length of the lane. Ginnie knew Toran would figure out a peaceful resolution to their predicament.

That knowledge allowed her to take in the brook that ran parallel to them and the flock of five white ducks that quacked playfully at each other. The smell of the growing corn and alfalfa mingled in the air. She began to embrace the pleasant feelings rushing through her and let out a contented sigh. She glanced at the waters rushing over rocks, splashing at the grasses growing on either side.

Maybe we can go wading in the creek after our chores are done. That would be a fun end to a frustrating day. This day can't possibly get any worse, right?

She scanned the view in front of her.

Her gaze stopped at the porch.

Dad sat on the concrete steps, elbows on his knees, his chin resting on folded, intertwined fingers. His eyes met hers. A chill slid down her spine.

CHAPTER THIRTY-SIX:
GROUNDED

D ad searched their faces as they approached.

Alarms in Ginnie's head went off. *Oh, snap! I forgot we're grounded. I wonder what chores he came up with.* "You ready for this?" Ginnie whispered to Toran.

"It doesn't matter. We're grounded until we do what he asks."

Ginnie turned to Tillie. "At least *you're* not in trouble."

Tillie shrugged, glancing between the three of them.

"Hi guys. Glad you're home." Dad stood and held out his hands. "I'll take your backpacks. Toran and Ginnie do your chores and then meet me in the living room."

"Yes, sir." They handed over their backpacks.

Oh great, the living room. More like the "stop having fun" room. Ginnie grimaced. The living room was pleasant enough, but she often found herself on the wrong end of a lecture there, so she preferred to avoid it when she could. *At least Toran'll get lectured too, for once.*

Dad hitched a thumb toward the barn. "See you when your chores are done." All three kids turned to go. Dad cleared his throat. "Tillie, I'd liked to speak with you for a minute … on the swing, please."

Tillie threw Ginnie a questioning look.

Ginnie didn't know what to say, so she offered a quick shrug, then smiled encouragingly at her friend.

Toran glanced at Dad, who nodded up the hill.

"We better get to it, Gin." Toran shrugged at Tillie, swiveled to the barn, and rushed ahead. Ginnie followed, but didn't quite catch up to him.

CHAPTER THIRTY-SEVEN:
A DREAM COME
TRUE ... SORTA

Ginnie and Toran rushed to the barn, leaving Tillie alone with their dad. Normally she wouldn't mind, but a weird feeling swept over her, not sure what to expect from his request. He offered an encouraging smile and motioned to the front porch swing.

Tillie climbed the four concrete steps, eyeing the wooden swing carefully. She sat on the end farthest from the door, sinking into the three-inch blue and white gingham foam cushion, her hands sliding nervously down her black jeans. "Am I in trouble?"

D.T. sat beside her, far enough away to leave a few inches gap. The space was reassuring somehow. He twisted to face her better. "I'm not sure yet. Why don't you tell me what happened at the movies yesterday."

Her heart thumped loudly in her chest.

She'd never been in trouble with him before. And she didn't want to be in trouble with him now.

Sucking in a quick breath to calm her growing anxiety, Tillie tried to focus on the tone of his voice. It wasn't harsh or sharp like Jasper's, her birth father's.

"D.T.'s not *him*," she scolded herself. *HE won't hurt me.*

D.T., which stood for 'Daddy Todd', the secret name she had called him forever, but just in her mind. On a summer day very much like today about four years ago, D.T. had held her on this very swing, after she'd scraped her knee, and reassured her that she'd be fine.

That day, she gave up hoping Jasper would return and be the nice dad to her that D.T. was to Ginnie. That day, she decided she'd pretend that D.T. was her own dad as well as her best friend's. He didn't make her feel like she had to be invisible to be loved. And now that D.T. was dating her mom, she would only have to pretend a little while longer.

Soon he would be her dad … *for real.*

"I-I'm sorry we didn't tell you, we … I … " Tillie dropped her face into her hands, unable to look at him.

He slid his arm around her shoulder and gave her a quick hug. "It's okay, Tillie. I'm not mad at you."

"You're not?" Her heart quickened its beat.

"No, but we still have a problem. I'd appreciate it if you would help me solve it." His quiet words soothed the familiar anxiety threatening to overwhelm her.

"What kind of problem?"

"The kind of problem that is new to both of us." He waited until she met his gaze, his eyes kind.

Her brows knit in confusion. Her thoughts raced to figure out what he was talking about.

"Until now you've always been Ginnie's friend, as well as the rest of our family's. You know the rules around here as well as my kids and you're good at following them, sometimes even better than Ginnie." He chuckled softly. "Well, quite often better than Ginnie."

Heat rose to Tillie's cheeks. She ducked her head.

He lifted her chin with a gentle finger. "But now I'm dating your mom and that complicates things *today*. The problem is that I've never been a stepdad before. But since I've been like a stepson, I want to make this easy for you."

Stepdad? He's gonna marry Mom? For real?

Silent, happy squeals drowned out his next words.

" … you know my folks died in a car accident and I came here to live with Uncle Ben and Aunt Sadie when I was eleven, right?"

Tillie nodded.

"It took a while to adjust to my folks dying and that I now had two new sets of parents to get used to."

"*Two* sets of parents?"

"Yes, when Jake and I moved in, Oma and Opa still lived here.

Uncle Ben was our guardian, but he and his parents ran the farm together back then. Then Oma's hay fever got too bad and Uncle Eli built them a house on his property. They moved there when I was seventeen."

Tillie had been to Oma and Opa's house a couple of times, but mostly Ginnie's great-grandparents came to the farm to visit for special occasions—like the twins' birthday last week. Oma and Opa always brought a gift for her birthday as well. Not always as fancy as what they brought Ginnie and Toran, but that didn't matter, they *always* remembered her.

"I talked with your mom this morning and she was surprised to find out that you, Toran, and Ginnie had been in a second fight with Pierce."

"But I couldn't tell—" Tillie started to protest, then clamped her mouth shut, not wanting to rat out her friends.

"You promised Ginnie and Toran not to tell me?"

She didn't need to respond. Her flaming cheeks broadcast her guilt.

"That's what I figured. Which is *another* problem."

Her insides twisted. *Please don't hate me.*

"My kids are in trouble because they hid that from me. And the irony is … I don't think they really did anything else wrong." His soft tone didn't soothe the forming knots. "Ginnie and Toran swear it was self-defense and from what I could gather, *you* were just in the wrong place at the wrong time."

Tillie glanced up quickly, then concentrated on his boots.

He paused a second before continuing. "Pierce is a pretty big guy. Funny how people can be braver for a friend than themselves."

Tillie swallowed hard enough to hear her ears pop.

"So now I learn all *three* of you are equally guilty about not telling me. How do you think I should handle that?"

The question wasn't angry, and yet panic rose. *He's gonna hate me forever now.* She shrugged, trying to figure out how to fix this.

"I try to make it a policy to get input from my kids as to why something did or didn't happen, before I decide on a consequence. This is your opportunity to let me know *your* thoughts."

MY kids? He thinks I'm one of HIS kids? She snapped her eyes to his, joy-filled bubbles swallowing the rising panic. "Ummm." No good reason came to mind.

"Take your time." He looked at his watch, then back at her. "You have a few minutes before Ginnie and Toran are done with their chores."

"I don't know what to say."

"Then please answer a couple of questions for me." He waited for her to nod. "Did you start the fight?"

She shook her head.

"Could you have avoided the fight?"

"I don't think so. Pierce went straight for Ginnie and Toran. I don't think he cared about me being there, until I told Ginnie to ignore him. Then he got mad."

"I see. Then why keep it a secret?"

"Because we didn't think he'd tell anybody and Ginnie didn't want to paint the fence again."

A small smile crossed his lips before his face became serious. "Well, if you guys had let me know what happened yesterday, I don't think there would have been a reason to consequence you at all. But I don't like being deceived."

His last words cut through her. "But that's not what we meant to do. We didn't want to worry you or Mom."

"Maybe not. Put yourself in my place. How do you think I felt when Pierce's dad accused you guys of beating his kid up? I didn't want to believe it, but I saw Pierce, *with a black eye*. If one of you had let me know what happened, I would've been better prepared to deal with that."

Guilt mingled with anxiety. Her joy-filled bubbles burst all at once. He'd never be able to forgive her now. Tillie dropped her head into her hands.

"Tilda?"

"Yes?" She opened her fingers a crack to peek at his face. He didn't look mad. Instead, he looked both puzzled *and* amused. She didn't expect that. *Where's the anger?*

"I talked with your mom a little while ago. She thinks that since the *three* of you decided together to keep this from us, the *three* of you should get the same consequence. How do you feel about that?"

She lowered her hands. "That seems fair."

"Okay then, consider yourself an official West kid today." He winked at her. "Or a Taylor-West."

"*Just* West is fine." Happiness surged through her. She giggled when she realized that although she just got promoted to being a full West, she was also about to be busted, just like Ginnie.

But that knowledge didn't lessen her good feelings.

D.T. chuckled and stood. "Come on. Let's go get a cookie before I have to be the bad guy."

Tillie followed him to the front door, not even caring that he was going to punish her.

She was just happy to be a *real* West... *finally*.

CHAPTER THIRTY-EIGHT: NOT LETTING BY-GONES BE BY-GONES

Bandit wolfed down the dog food that popped out of his bowl while Ginnie filled it in the main barn. She dropped the scoop in the plastic container and pushed the lid down. After plucking up his silver-gray cat, Princess, and draping her like a scarf over his shoulders, Toran climbed up the wooden ladder to check on her five newborn kittens.

"Aw man! She moved them again. Do you know where the kittens are?" Toran called, leaning over a hay bale stacked near the edge of the loft. He now had Princess in his arms, petting her.

A light spray of green alfalfa dust rained from above.

"I have no idea. Sorry." Ginnie's thoughts were focused on what would be in the lecture they were going to get.

More chores, I bet ... and hard ones. This is all Pierce's fault. Dad's tale about chores he had to do as a kid weighed on her. She didn't want to paint another *anything* for a good long time. Doing dishes for a week started to sound better to her, at least that wasn't hours of work in the same day.

"I'm gonna do the chickens now," Ginnie said.

"I'll get to the hogs in a minute. I want to find the babies."

"Okay." Ginnie kicked a straw bale and stormed down the hill to the pasture behind the farmhouse.

The more she thought about Pierce threatening her, the angrier she became. She didn't want to think about making posters with

Pierce, ice cream sandwiches, or not.

Her mind turned to Toran and Austin's list of pranks to motivate Pierce to behave. The burning bags of cow manure seemed like a better idea all the time … that and public humiliation. She rubbed her wrist. No way was she going to let Pierce get away with intimidating her.

She continued to stew about Pierce's threat as she fed the chickens. She didn't pay attention to the first scoop of cracked corn she poured and half of it missed its mark from the long slender feeding troughs, skittering about the dirt where impatient hens ate greedily.

She paid better attention when she scooped more feed. After filling the automatic waterer, Ginnie replaced the yellow hose, then glanced around the coop for the few eggs she might find. There were three. Two brown and one white. She'd already gathered a basketful this morning.

Ginnie met Toran coming out of the hog barn. "So, how're we going to deal with Pierce?"

"What do you think about asking Dad to take us to Pierce's and work out something with him off school property? If you let me do the talking, maybe we can avoid another fight."

"Puh-lease. That's almost as bad as going to his mom and tattling." She held her fingers up to air quote. "And 'talking' last night didn't go so well. Let's burn Trixie's manure. And make a PA announcement saying Pierce sucks his thumb and sleeps with a blanky. A pink one, because his parents really wanted a girl."

Toran laughed. "Are you feeling a tad hateful?"

"A little." Ginnie smirked while toggling her head. "Aren't you glad I'm not mad at *you* anymore?"

Toran shrugged. "I'm not worried about you, but it sounds like Pierce should be."

Ginnie rolled her eyes. "You grab my arm again like you did earlier, and I'll give you a reason to change your mind."

"Oh, yeah. You really scare me." Toran's mocking tone grated on her nerves. He continued in his normal voice. "Dad'll be waiting. Are you about done?"

"Yeah. I just need to drop the eggs off in the kitchen."

Toran glanced at his watch. "Dad'll probably milk Gertrude after he lectures us—unless you smart off to him. Then he'll have *you* do it."

"You're such a comedian." But Ginnie knew he was right. She tried not to groan, hoping Dad wouldn't say something that would make her want to scream.

Toran buffed the nails of his right hand on his red t-shirt and laughed. "Some days."

Ginnie grimaced.

Toran held the side porch door open. "Whatever. But I bet you get 'the look' more than I do. Take some advice." He blocked the doorway and lowered his voice. "Never pass up a chance to keep your mouth shut. Dad likes to think we're actually thinking about what he says. When you argue with him, he *knows* you're not paying attention. Don't be so obvious and your grounding might end today—as promised."

Ginnie marveled at the sneakiness of his advice. Since he never got in as much trouble as she did, it seemed like a good idea to at least consider his words.

But that didn't mean she had to show her appreciation right away. No sense puffing up his ego more than necessary.

They met Dad and Tillie in the living room. The lecture itself went quickly. After pointing out that he was grounding them because they hid the fight with Pierce from him, Dad wagged his finger at each of them, leaving it pointed at Ginnie a little longer. "That had better never happen again. If you get in another fight or do something else you shouldn't, I better hear about it from *you*. Is that understood?"

Each nodded. "Yes, sir."

Ginnie was surprised at how enthusiastic Tillie sounded. She didn't seem the least bit bothered at getting lectured.

"Good. It'll be your job to sweep, mop, and vacuum every floor in the house as well as dust all the wooden furniture. When you're done, so is your grounding."

Toran and Ginnie exchanged relieved looks.

"Yes, sir. I'll be happy to."

Tillie chimed in on the "yes sir," but looked puzzled at the 'I'll be happy too.'

Toran filled her in on Dad's deal from last night.

The twitch of Dad's lip gave away his humor. "Let me know when you're done. I have to work on the farm books. Do your best."

They went room by room, vacuuming, sweeping, mopping, and

dusting as needed.

Miss Amanda showed up just before they were done.

"Toran and I can finish up," Ginnie offered, feeling bad about Tillie getting busted as well.

"No. It was my fault too. I earned the same punishment and I'm going to finish."

"I bet Dad won't care," Ginnie said.

Tillie planted her hands on her hips. "*I* care."

Ginnie did a double-take at her tone, surprised at how determined she sounded. "Fine, we're about done anyway."

Dad and Miss Amanda talked on the front porch swing while they finished their assigned tasks. Tillie made sure every speck of dust was lifted from every piece of furniture. She was worse than Toran, and he was crazy neat like Dad. Finally, they finished.

After doing a quick inspection, Dad approved their work and pronounced their grounding over. Tillie beamed when he thanked her for doing a great job.

Ginnie thought her friend took the grounding too well, but wasn't sorry that Miss Amanda had to rush off with Tillie before long.

She had a plan to get Pierce back and Tillie would just get in the way.

CHAPTER THIRTY-NINE:
THE PHONE

After Dad walked Miss Amanda to her car and went back into the study, Ginnie stopped Toran in the upstairs hallway. "Tor, call Austin and see if Pete Jr. can still take us to Pierce's."

"I can't. Uncle Ben's making dinner in the kitchen and Dad's in the study. No phones."

"There's one in Dad's room. Use that one."

"You know we're not allowed in there without permission."

"Quit being a worrywart. *I'll* get you the phone. You can call Austin in your room."

Toran shook his head. "There's a lot of sneaking going on. Dad just said he doesn't want to be blindsided again. We just "yes sir-red"him. That means we gave our word. Now we're sneaking again. I'm not so okay with this."

Ginnie held up her wrist. "I'm not so okay with this."

Before Toran could protest, she pushed him toward his room. "Go on." He paused, and then shook his head.

Ginnie held up her wrist again.

Grimacing, Toran glanced at her wrist and headed toward his room.

Ginnie tiptoed over to the front window. Uncle Jake's truck was still gone, as was Buzz's truck and Vi's VW bug. She stepped quickly to Dad's bedroom door and turned the knob. Excitement pulsed through her.

She glanced around the hallway and slipped inside Dad and Uncle

Jake's room. She had been in the room many times, but she always smiled when she saw how neat her dad's side was compared to her uncle's. Not that Uncle Jake was a super slob, but his bed was always more wrinkled and his dresser more cluttered. And his chair was always draped with clothes.

Her own room was neater than Uncle Jake's side, but that was because Dad never granted privileges if he knew her room was a mess, *not* because she followed in his neat freak footsteps like Toran.

She snatched the phone from its charger and headed back to Toran's room.

CHAPTER FORTY:
THE CALL

O nce Ginnie handed him Dad's phone, Toran waved toward
her room. She opened her mouth to protest, but walked
over to her door instead.

He pointed again to her room.

"Why can't I hear?"

He stretched to his tallest height. "Do you want me to call him
or not?"

"Whatever!" She flounced into her room. "I'll get my backpack
and pack what we need."

Toran waited for her door to close. He didn't need her two cents
while talking with Austin.

Maybe if Austin caved, they wouldn't have to go through with
this. All the sneaking was getting to him. Dad had seemed madder at
Ginnie last night, but if they got caught tonight, Toran was pretty
sure *he'd* get the worst of whatever punishment Dad came up with.

That didn't happen often and Toran sure didn't want it to
happen now. He and Dad had an unspoken agreement.. If Toran
knew about Ginnie's crazy plans, it was his job to redirect her, not
encourage her penchant for trouble.

Just when Toran thought nobody was home, Austin picked up.
Dung beetles. "Hi, Austin."

"Toran! Oh, good! Are we still on tonight? Pete Jr.'s looking
forward to it."

Great! So much for ditching.

"Yeah, we're on." Toran scanned his brain for a way out.

Nothing popped into his head.

"I can't believe you're coming along. You never do anything wrong." Austin cackled as he teased. "Welcome to the dark side."

Toran winced at the backhanded compliment. "Very funny."

"Sorry, but this isn't like you."

"Yeah, well. This is what Pierce gets for threatening Ginnie. I have to look out for her, right?"

"When did he threaten her? To hear Ginnie tell it, she nailed *him* at the movies."

"He twisted her wrist after school today and promised to pay her back. I can't let that happen, now can I?" Toran was almost happy Pierce threatened Ginnie when he heard Austin suck in an angry breath.

"Pierce threatened her? What a jerk! He's twice her size and she's a *girl!*"

"I know, she's *my* sister."

Awesome. Bonus cool points with Austin!

"She asked me to help, so I told her I'd take care of it. When's Pete Jr. getting home from work?"

"About seven-fifteen."

"Good. Tell him we're on." Toran hung up and swallowed hard, his insides twisting like a winding mountain road.

CHAPTER FORTY-ONE:
OPERATION: FIREBALL

Toran swerved around Dad, nearly toppling his armful of dirty dishes to the kitchen floor.

"Where's the fire?" Dad asked.

"Nowhere." Ginnie took the dishes from Toran and set them in the sudsy water. "We just want to get done and go to Austin's. It's only an hour and a half before dark."

"Well, if it's that important, I can drive you." Dad glanced from one to the other.

The color drained from Toran's face.

Great, he's gonna pass out. Ginnie plopped the dishes in the hot, soapy water, relieved she had an excuse to turn from her dad's gaze. "No thanks. We're exercising Calliope as well. We had to do the floors, remember? I didn't get a chance to ride her."

"It's for school, right? I can finish the dishes for you. You did a great job on the floors."

Aw man! Her heartbeat quickened. Certain Dad could hear the loud thudding, she tossed the washcloth at Toran. "Table, please."

Toran caught the rag. "Uh, yeah."

Ginnie turned from him. *Real smooth, bro.* She snuck a peek at Dad.

He sat on a barstool. His eyes narrowed, but he didn't say anything. Toran walked into the dining room. Ginnie scrubbed the plates with a sponge and rinsed them before adding the glasses to the dishwater.

By the time Toran returned with the washcloth, only the pots remained. Ginnie scrubbed them as well. "Go saddle Calliope, I'm almost done."

"I did offer to finish the dishes for you," Dad reminded her.

"I know, but I only have a couple left and my hands are already wet." Ginnie glanced at her brother. "Tor, don't forget your backpack."

"Oh, yeah." Toran smiled at their dad and went out the side porch door.

Dad chuckled. "Okay. Remind me to help you again. You make it so easy."

Ginnie focused on the sink. *Only so I don't have to feel guilty for sneaking around you.*

The 'honesty' lecture nagged at her. She pulled the plug and sprayed the sinks clean. After she wrung out the washcloth, she laid it across the sink divider and dried her hands with a blue dishtowel.

Dad watched her every move.

"I'm done. See you around eight-thirty, okay?" She kissed his cheek without waiting for an answer, and rushed through the side porch.

"Be safe. I love you."

The words reached her just as she opened the second porch door. The wooden door slammed shut. She dashed up the hill, hoping to outrun her growing guilt.

Toran offered her a hand when Ginnie reached him and Calliope. She swung up behind him, getting a chest full of his backpack and a nose full of manure scent.

Toran grinned. "No last minute instructions?"

"Just a 'be safe. I love you'."

He grimaced. "Ouch. You want to back out?"

"No. But I want you to hand me your backpack. Pew!" Ginnie pinched her nostrils together.

Toran slid it off his shoulders. "Matches?"

"In my pocket." She slipped her arms into the straps of the backpack. "Let's go."

Toran gave Calliope a gentle kick and in no time they were at Chandler's Crossing.

Austin jogged over to them when they approached his house. "Let's put Calliope in the barn. Pete Jr. will be home soon."

They stabled Calliope in the stall next to Traxx. The horses neighed greetings to each other.

Austin pulled out his list. "Burn bags of manure. What about toilet papering the yard?"

Toran shook his head. "Not in the daylight."

"Good—'cause we need to buy more." Austin threw them a relieved smile. "My mom would notice if we took too many rolls right now."

Toran backed up a little and rubbed his hands on his blue jeans.

Ginnie could tell his nerves were kicking in. "Remember my wrist? He deserves this and more."

Austin glared. "We'll take care of him." Austin's tone almost matched the spite in Pierce's earlier and caused Ginnie to take a closer look at him.

His protectiveness irritated her. "I'm the same girl who knocked him on his rear twice. Of course he's mad. But *he* started it, so we're just gonna finish it."

"I know you're tough, Ginnie—but you're still a girl. And he's bigger than you." Austin's cheeks reddened. He turned to Toran for support. "That's just wrong."

"How do you think I feel? She's *my* twin sister." The bravado in Toran's voice seemed to cover what looked like second thoughts. He tucked his shirt into his jeans and nodded toward the lane. "There's Pete. Let's go."

Ginnie pressed her lips together, realizing just in time that Toran was justifying why he was going along, as practical jokes didn't sit well with him.

She turned to Austin. "Do you need to say goodbye to your folks?"

He nodded and ran to the minivan. He and Pete Jr. talked a minute. Austin followed his brother into the house after motioning for Ginnie and Toran to get into the van.

"This is exciting. We haven't done something like this in a long time." Ginnie hardly noticed that Toran didn't respond to her chatter.

Austin and Pete Jr. came back.

Pete Jr. turned in his seat to face them. He had brown hair like his dad and the same blue eyes as Austin, who looked more like their mom with his dark blond hair. "We got everything we need?"

Toran opened his backpack. "Sure. Bags, patties, matches. We just need to make a plan about who does what and when."

Austin leaned over. "I want to set a bag on fire."

"Me too," Ginnie and Toran said together and then added, "rock, paper, scissors," at the exact same moment.

Austin laughed. "Must be a twin thing."

"One, two, three." Ginnie made a scissor with her fingers and Toran formed a fist. "Rock beats scissors. You get to ring the doorbell while Austin and I light the bags."

"Fine." Excitement surged through Ginnie. She was glad Toran was on board. The last time she and Austin pulled a prank, he refused to go along.

When they neared Pierce's street, Pete Jr. pulled over, just around the corner from Pierce's house, where the mini-van wouldn't be seen.

"I have to stay with the van. You guys stick to the bushes. Light the bags where they won't catch anything on fire … like on rocks or concrete or something. When the bag catches, you two run while Ginnie rings the doorbell. Try not to trip over each other."

"Like we would," Austin scoffed.

Pete Jr. threw him a smirk. "How many times have you done this? Coordinate your efforts—it'll go better." He held out a hand. Each added a hand to the stack. "One, two, three. Go team."

They exchanged conspiratorial grins.

The boys each snatched a brown paper sack and Ginnie handed over the matches. "I only grabbed one pack. Sorry."

Austin shrugged. "No prob. We'll light them together."

Toran raised a hand. "There's a mom pushing a stroller. She'll go by soon."

When the street cleared, they approached Pierce's house and hid behind the bushes in his side yard.

Ginnie's heart pounded with excitement.

Toran swallowed and nodded at her. "You go first. Hunker down near the doorbell, once we toss the bags, ring the bell and run. *Fast.*"

"Wait, what's the porch made of?" Austin peeked around the bushes. "Cement. We're good."

"All clear?" Toran asked.

Austin nodded.

"Wish me luck then. I'll get closer and give you a 'thumbs up' to light the sacks." Ginnie exchanged a fist bump with each boy and crept toward the house.

A loud TV show punctuated the air. *At least they won't hear me.* She paused by the garage before going to the porch. The front door was only a little ajar.

Good, they won't see me. She took a breath and exhaled, her hands trembling. *Get a grip, Gin. It's just a 'ring and run'.* She stepped onto the porch and heard "No, Dad. I'm sorry! I'm sorry!"

Wow, that's a loud TV show.

"I told you to take out the trash," a man's angry voice yelled.

"Ray, he's doing it. Give him a minute." A woman's voice quivered in answer.

"Don't tell me how to raise my son!" THWACK.

Ginnie looked through the crack in the door. She heard a whimper. "Sorry, sorry."

A meaty hand flew through the air, connecting with the chest area of a yellow t-shirt. This thwack turned Ginnie's stomach. The T-shirt dropped to the floor like a dirty dishrag.

That's no TV show. That's Pierce's dad. Ginnie froze, her sneakers glued to the porch. Her mind screamed "Run!" but her feet wouldn't budge.

"Psst. Psst. Is it clear?"

Ginnie looked towards the bushes. Austin's face held a nervous smile while Toran lit a bag. She shook her head several times and made slashing motions with her hand.

Toran dropped the sack.

She continued to shake her head with much more animation. She made stomping motions with her foot a couple times and glued her eyes to the door.

"Get up!" Mr. Owens roared.

Ginnie stood still. *What do I do?*

A large workman's boot kicked into the lump of denim on the floor. "OW!" Louder whimpers.

Pierce scrambled to get up.

Ginnie's brain jumpstarted her body.

She banged on the door. "Don't hurt him!"

Loud footsteps stomped toward her.

CHAPTER FORTY-TWO:
BURNT TOAST

Chilled blood flooded Ginnie's limbs, freezing her in place.

"What are you doing?" Toran whispered loudly.

Ginnie snapped out of her trance and tore down the driveway. "Run—it's his dad." The three of them dashed up the sidewalk and around the corner. Ginnie reached the van first. She left the door open and hurried in. "Just sit next to me, Austin. Toran, get in the back!"

Toran slid into the seat behind her as Austin rushed in next to her. "Go, Pete! Go!"

"Are you crazy?" Austin demanded of Ginnie, pulling the door closed. "Go, Pete!"

Pete started the car and sped away. "Did they see you?"

Ginnie looked behind her. No sign of Pierce's dad. "I don't know." Her hands trembled.

"What happened? Why did you bang on the door?" Toran put his hand on her shoulder. "You look horrible. Why are you shaking?"

"It was awful, Tor! Pierce's dad. He knocked him down and then kicked his leg. Pierce was crying and so was his mom. It didn't matter. His dad kept hurting him."

Her legs began to shake.

Austin's eyes popped open wide. "No way!"

"Tell me you didn't throw the bags." Ginnie's gaze darted from Austin to Toran. "I don't want Pierce hurt more because of us."

"We didn't. I'm not sure I stomped the fire all the way out between the time you yelled at his dad and flew past us though. What were you thinking?" Toran demanded.

"I thought Pierce's dad was going to kill him, *for real*." Ginnie wiped at her eyes. "It was awful!"

"No wonder he's so mean." Austin slumped against the seat. "I don't feel so good."

"Did he see you, Gin? Does he know it was you guys?" Pete Jr.'s voice rose in pitch.

"I dunno," Austin replied.

"Me either. Once Ginnie ran to us—I tried to get the fire out and follow." Toran lifted his shoe, which had a burn mark on it.

"I told Mom we went for ice cream. Anybody feel like eating so I didn't lie?" Pete Jr. asked.

"No way." Ginnie's belly turned at the thought.

Toran moaned. "We're in deep. I don't know why I went along with this. Ginnie, stop crying."

Ginnie rubbed at her eyes, unaware she had tears on her cheeks. "I can't help it. Toran, his dad was s-o-o-o mad. Do you think he went back and hurt him more? Or stopped because he knew someone saw? Should we call the police? What do we do?" Her anxiety rose with each question.

Austin shrugged. "Maybe tell our folks?"

"Good thinking, pea-brain. Then we can get grounded for the rest of our lives." Pete Jr. tossed Austin a disgusted look. "And Dad'll take my license. *No way.*"

"Uncle Ben says we should do the right thing just because it's the right thing to do. Pierce could be in real trouble." Ginnie glanced around the car. "What if his dad keeps hurting him?"

"I'm sure his dad thinks we'll call the cops. He probably stopped hitting him." Toran sat up straighter. "At least I hope so. Dad's going to ground us for the rest of our lives. And he'll make painting the fences seem like an amusement park ride."

Ginnie shook her head. "He'll be mad, but he'll understand. The worst he'd ever do is swat us on the rear. And he hasn't done that in *forever*. He'd never punch us or kick us like a rabid dog. Or anything else." The image of Pierce curled on the floor absorbing several kicks was seared in her mind. She trembled.

"If you guys confess—we'll have to as well. Our dads are friends. Let's just call 9-1-1 on Pierce's dad and leave it alone," Pete Jr. advised.

"Well then … call 9-1-1." Austin spoke quickly. "That's the main thing, right? Helping Pierce?"

Pete Jr. handed Austin his cell phone. "You do it. I'm driving."

Austin stiffened.

Toran grabbed it out of his hand. "I'll do it." He dialed 9-1-1. "I'd like to report a kid being beat by his dad." Toran put his hand over the mouthpiece. "What's the address?"

"Jackson Street. No, drive. Jackson Drive. 325 or 235. I don't remember. Next door to a bright yellow house. Was their house brown or green?" They talked over each other.

Toran moved his hand. "It's a brown, one-story house. Three houses from the corner of Jackson and Washington. Next door to a bright yellow house. Right side facing north. Yes, ma'am. No, ma'am. Just hurry. The dad's a big guy. Ray Owens. Thank you." Toran clicked the phone. "It's a small street. They'll figure it out."

Toran gave the phone to Austin and sat back.

"Okay. Pierce's getting help. We'll be home in a minute. No harm, no foul. We can just pretend like it didn't happen. Agreed?" Pete Jr. clicked on the turn signal.

"We can be home before Dad suspects anything, Toran. What do you think?" Not confessing appealed to Ginnie. She turned to Toran. "No sense borrowing trouble, right?"

Toran bit his lip. "Only if Mr. Owens didn't see you. If he shows up again and we don't warn Dad, we'll be grounded until we're grandparents."

"That'll be a good trick, since you'd have to get married first—and not to each other. That'd be gross." Austin looked around, but nobody laughed at his joke.

Pete Jr. shook his head. "Give it up, bro. Guys we gotta agree. You ran fast, right? If he's a big guy—he probably didn't see you. Let's go with that, okay? I don't want to lose my driving privileges."

Austin, Toran, and Ginnie exchanged looks and shrugs. They each nodded their agreement.

"Three Musketeers?" Austin put his hand out.

Ginnie put hers on top of his. Then Toran. "Three Musketeers."

Pete Jr. cleared his throat. "Make that four. We're all in this together."

CHAPTER FORTY-THREE:
OOPS!

Ginnie and Toran made their way up the front porch steps, hoping to avoid any family members milling about the kitchen and family room at the other end of the house.

Toran opened the door for Ginnie. "Wash your face. You look like you've been crying.

Ginnie nodded as she walked past him.

Toran followed her up the stairs.

The study door flew open.

"Is there something you want to tell me?" Dad asked, a stern look on his face.

Ginnie's knees weakened as she turned, slumping to a sitting position on a step. *I've really done it this time.* Her guilt and anxiety loosened her tongue. "I'm so sorry, Daddy! We shouldn't have done it, but when Pierce hurt my wrist, I just wanted to get him back."

She stopped talking, choking on sobs, barely registering a puzzled look on Dad's face before her tears took over. "But then Pierce's dad …" She wiped furiously at her eyes. "Daddy, he really hurt him. We called 9-1-1, but …"

"What?" Dad hurried to the stairs. "What are you talking about? I was just teasing you. I thought you were sneaking off to bed without saying goodnight." His worried eyes locked on hers. "What about Pierce? And your arm? And 9-1-1?"

Sugar beets! Ginnie threw an apologetic look at Toran.

"It's okay Gin, we should tell him." Toran stood next to the wall. "Dad, it was my idea, well, Austin's, but I encouraged him."

Dad reached for Ginnie's hand. "What did Pierce do to you?"

Ginnie sniffed as Dad examined her wrist. "It's nothing, Daddy. But we went to his house ..."

"On Calliope?" The anger in his voice alarmed her.

She and Toran shook their heads. "Pete Jr. drove us."

"What?!"

Ginnie snatched her hand back and covered her face.

Uncle Ben walked up behind Dad. "Is everything all right?"

"No, sir. I'm trying to figure what's going on." Dad motioned both kids to the living room. "Now."

Ginnie stood and followed closely behind Toran as he walked down the stairs.

"You can bust us later, Dad." Toran stopped in front of their dad. "Pierce might be in real trouble."

Dad pointed at the living room door, his tone softening. "I'm listening."

After Ginnie and Toran sat on the couch, Toran filled him in: on the prank, Ginnie seeing Mr. Owens beat Pierce, their run for cover, and calling 9-1-1.

Dad's face ran the gamut of surprise, anger, shock, and other emotions.

Uncle Ben found his voice first. "9-1-1 would have to follow up, especially with a kid involved. Does Ray know you saw?"

Ginnie shrugged and looked at Toran.

"We don't know. We ran like crazy. He's too big to chase anybody, but if he saw us, he knows where we live." Toran slapped his leg. "Aw man, I didn't think of that."

Ginnie's stomach lurched. "Me either."

Uncle Ben looked at his watch. "When did this happen?"

Toran shrugged. "A little bit ago. Pete Jr. took us back to Chandler's Crossing. We got on Calliope and rode home."

Uncle Ben stood. "All right. Todd, you drive. The police will still be there if it just happened."

"Drive where?" Ginnie's panicked eyes connected with Dad's, before glancing at her great-uncle.

Uncle Ben pointed at the door. "The Owens.' I'm going to presume he saw you. If he's going to treat his own kid like that, I want to know he won't be thinking you're next. Marsha is going to be out of her mind with fear. She used to be in my Sunday school class years ago. I think she might let me help her."

Dad shook his head. "I don't want them anywhere near Ray."

"Me either." Toran added, shaking his head as well.

"They'll be staying in the car. Ginnie is a witness and needs to give a statement. After the mess with Jasper and Amanda, we can't ignore this."

Uncle Ben gave Dad 'the look'.

"Uncle Ben, if Ray hurt Pierce, what's to stop him from going after *my* kids?" Dad shook his head harder. "I'm not sure I see the wisdom in that, if he didn't see them. No sense borrowing trouble."

"Do what you like then. I'm going to help Marsha and Pierce." Uncle Ben turned toward the door.

"I didn't say I wouldn't go." Dad motioned for Ginnie and Toran to follow as he caught up to Uncle Ben. "I'm just saying I'm not sure I want my kids over there."

"Understood. But I'm going."

"Going where?" Uncle Jake asked as he, Buzz, and Vi entered the front door.

"Ray's. He just beat up Pierce," Dad said.

Vi's hand flew to her mouth.

Uncle Jake arched an eyebrow. "How do you know?"

Dad grimaced. "Because your niece and nephew just pranked their house and Ginnie saw him."

Uncle Jake's smile only stayed long enough for Dad's words to sink in. "That can't be good."

"Ya think?" Dad pulled his keys out of his pocket. "Stay with them while Uncle Ben and I figure out what's going on."

"Heck no. I'm coming with you." Uncle Jake opened the screen door. "Buzz, stay with the kids."

"Hey …" Buzz protested.

"If Uncle Jake's coming, I want to go too." Ginnie looked at Dad. "Uncle Ben says I should."

"You didn't want to a minute ago," Dad reminded her.

"That was before I knew Uncle Jake was coming. He'll *punch* Mr. Owens if he causes trouble."

"Which is why we're leaving the hotheads at home. You too." Dad raised a determined brow first at Uncle Jake and then Ginnie. "Stay."

"I have my own truck." Uncle Jake jangled his keys. "You're my *little* brother and it's still my job to look out for you. Get over it."

Ginnie smiled and reached for Uncle Jake's hand. "Can I ride with you?"

"Sure."

"No ma'am. You're staying here." Dad wagged a warning finger.

"But Uncle Ben ..."

"*Isn't* your father." Dad stood straighter. "*I am.*"

Uncle Jake threw her a sympathetic look as he shrugged.

"But he said I should tell the police ..."

Uncle Jake winked at her. "That's true, Todd. As a witness, she should come."

"Are you listening to yourself, Jacob?" Vi scolded as she pulled Ginnie into a hug. "Ray beat up Pierce, so you think we should take Ginnie and Toran over there as well? You're certifiable."

Ginnie broke out of the hug. "But I want to go. Uncle Jake'll keep me safe."

"No way. You're staying here ... with me." Vi threw Dad a determined glance. "Tell her, Todd."

Ginnie's heart fell to her toes. With Vi on Dad's side, she knew she wouldn't be allowed to come.

"Dad?" Toran locked his eyes on their dad's. "I know we're in a hurry, but please hear me out."

Dad started to shake his head, but stopped. "Make it quick."

Toran swallowed. "Pierce needs a friend. Maybe we can help. Please let us go."

Seconds of silence passed. Dad pointed his finger at Ginnie. "Virginia Maie, *you* will ride with me and you *will* stay in the car unless I say otherwise, understood?"

"Yes, sir." Ginnie bit her cheek to keep from smiling.

"Toran, you're with me as well. You can tell me what happened and we'll figure out what to do on the way. After this mess gets settled." Dad sent each a warning look. "We'll be talking about your unauthorized field trip."

"Yes, sir," both replied and followed him out.

"I'm coming too," Buzz said.

Uncle Jake held up his keys. "I've got room."

CHAPTER FORTY-FOUR:
BORROWING TROUBLE

Innie's belly twisted and turned, alternating between excitement and dread as they neared Pierce's house.

"Oh my goodness!" The words escaped in a horrified gasp as she noted the street crawling with police cars and an ambulance. A fire truck drove away as they pulled up.

Dad parked two houses away on the opposite side of the street. He took the key out of the ignition and turned to Ginnie. "Stay put. You're in enough trouble."

She ducked her head. "Yes, sir."

"You too." Dad sent a glance Toran's way as he twisted to leave the car.

"Yes, sir."

After a final stern look, Dad rolled down his window and shut his door.

Uncle Ben followed suit. "Mind your dad. We'll be back when we know what's going on."

Ginnie and Toran leaned back against the seat and looked at one another.

Toran sighed. "At least the call helped."

"Yeah, but I want to see." Ginnie climbed through the middle to the driver's seat.

She jolted when the door opened.

Uncle Jake's smiling face appeared. He seemed to enjoy knowing he startled her. "You'll get a better view from my truck."

"Dad said to stay here," Toran reminded them both.

"He meant … don't go near the house—and my truck is farther away than his car."

Ginnie scrambled out the door. "Thanks, Uncle Jake."

He put a hand on her shoulder. His face turned serious. "Stay in it so I don't catch trouble from your dad. Understood?"

"Yes, sir."

"Do you want me to take back my offer?" Uncle Jake furrowed his brow. "Don't 'sir' me."

"Sorry. Daddy just used that same voice to lecture us."

He chuckled. "I'll forgive you then. Don't make me regret it. I left the windows down."

"We won't." Ginnie wiggled her eyebrows at Buzz and Vi as she rushed by them to Uncle Jake's truck. She opened the door and climbed up the running board. *Uncle Jake was right; I have a much better view from up here.*

Toran followed a minute later.

"I knew you'd come." Ginnie played with the steering wheel until it locked in place. "Sugar beets."

"And I knew *you'd* need a babysitter." Toran hitched a thumb towards Dad. "Uncle Jake's getting an earful about it already."

Ginnie leaned closer to the windshield. Dad pointed at Uncle Jake in a scolding manner, then back at the truck. Ginnie slid down the seat.

Uncle Jake just shrugged.

Uncle Ben approached an officer talking with a man and woman standing at the edge of the driveway where Toran and Austin had lit the bags on fire. They couldn't see if the bags were still there.

Dad, Uncle Jake, Vi, and Buzz joined him.

"We kicked the bags under the bushes, they're probably hidden," Toran said.

There were several small groups of people gathered in clumps, talking in the yards surrounding the Owens' house. Their eyes darted between the house and the police cars.

Ginnie saw movement in the police car closest to her. "Toran, it's Pierce's dad!"

"No way." Toran moved forward. "It is. I hope he stopped hurting Pierce before they got here."

"Me, too." The thought sobered her. "Toran, Pierce has got to be scared … and embarrassed. What do you think will happen to him?"

Toran shrugged. "I don't know. But look." He pointed at a police officer walking towards the car with Pierce's dad in it. He opened the driver's door and signaled to another officer, who hurried to the squad car in front of him. Both officers got in their cars and drove away.

After they left, another police man approached Uncle Ben. Dad and Vi followed them into the Owens' house while Uncle Jake and Buzz continued to talk with the neighbors.

"I wish we could get out. Mr. Owens is gone." Ginnie sat against the gray cloth bench seat.

"Me too, but don't. We're still in trouble for sneaking over here in the first place. With a little luck, Dad'll forget about us and worry more about Pierce."

They sat for a few minutes counting people. The clumps of onlookers dwindled. Ginnie leaned her forehead on the steering wheel. "I wonder how much longer we have to wait."

"Not much. Dad's coming."

Ginnie perched upright, her heartbeat quickening. She waited until he got closer to open the door.

"Scoot over, please."

Ginnie moved over as Dad slid in next to her.

Toran leaned forward to see around Ginnie. "What's going on?"

"Pierce and his mom are inside with Uncle Ben and Vi. Pierce is having a hard time. I thought about what you said. He could use a friend." His gaze rested on Ginnie. "He's still mad about you decking him, but if you can ignore his bad attitude, maybe he can move past that."

Toran and Ginnie exchanged looks and shrugs. Toran spoke first. "Do you want to?"

Ginnie nodded, slanting a glance at Dad. "How mad is he? Does he know I saw?"

Dad exhaled and sat back in the seat. "Yeah, and so does Ray. He saw you running down the street. I don't think he knows why you were here though, and no one has asked. I told Pierce I know he twisted your wrist and made it clear to him that it had better not happen again."

Ginnie smiled. "What did he say to that?"

"Nothing, he just scowled." Dad turned on his "lecture voice," smirking. "I also told him I would be having a discussion with you two and assured him you would be greatly motivated to avoid him in the future if the three of you don't come to an understanding. He perked up a little."

Her smile fled.

Dad cleared his throat. "Do you want to see him?"

She nodded. "Sure."

"Me too," Toran said.

"Okay." Dad ran his hand through his hair and then pointed his finger at Ginnie. "Don't make me regret this. You're still in the doghouse with me."

She dropped her gaze to his cowboy boots. "Yes, sir." She followed him out of the truck.

CHAPTER FORTY-FIVE:
BEFRIENDING PIERCE

Dad stopped walking when they reached the porch. He put a firm hand on each of their shoulders. "You don't have to do this, if you really don't want to."

Toran took a breath and exhaled. "I know, but we owe him. Even though *he* started it."

Ginnie blew her bangs out of her eyes and steeled her wobbly nerves. "We need to help … if we can."

The humidity hadn't lifted much, even though dusk had fallen and the street lights had turned on a while ago.

"I'm here for you." Dad pulled each of them into a quick hug. "Pierce is angry and in really bad shape. I know I can count on you to be sensitive to what he must be feeling. He's really defensive, so don't take anything he says personally."

Ginnie nodded. "We won't."

Dad lowered his voice. "Maybe you could invite him out to the farm to make ice cream or something fun. He could really use something else to think about right now. He's scared about his dad being arrested and what Ray'll do to him when he gets out of jail."

That reality was a little too much for Ginnie. All her anger toward Pierce turned into a lead ball in her middle. Remembering her angry proclamation to Mrs. Johnson about Pierce being a jerk, sickened her.

Why hadn't she realized *WHY* Pierce was such a bully? She hadn't had much sympathy for him when his dad had been so mean at the farm. She had *chosen* to stay angry with him because he hurt Tillie.

Dad lifted her chin. "Are you okay, Gin?"

She nodded, suddenly grateful that the man who stood before her was the man *she* got to call 'Dad'.

Poor Pierce.

"What should we say?" Toran asked.

"It would probably be best if you let *him* do most of the talking and if all else fails, apologize. If you take more responsibility for this mess, he can save face. And speaking of faces—his is really bruised. Try not to look shocked when you see him. He's a little sensitive about it."

"Sure, Dad." Toran took a step forward, leading the way through the front door.

Ginnie didn't see her brother stop. She walked straight into him, then sucked in a loud breath when she spotted Pierce, who sat between his mom and Uncle Ben on the sofa. Vi sat next to Mrs. Owens on a dining room chair.

Vi gave a slight shake of her head when she met Ginnie's gaze.

Ginnie closed her mouth, stunned. *Dad wasn't kidding.*

Pierce's face looked like a multi-colored balloon, mostly red, black, and purple, with a little green and yellow thrown in for good measure. The cheek opposite of his black eye now sported a growing bruise. Three horizontal lines imprinted on the swollen red cheek.

Ginnie's stomach lurched in horrified realization … pressure marks from his father's fingers. Fuzzy white noise buzzed in her ears while she gulped for air.

She grasped Toran's arms to steady herself, before she stepped to his side.

When Pierce caught sight of them, his signature scowl replaced the tentative smile he had worn for Uncle Ben.

A few seconds of uncomfortable silence passed.

Uncle Ben stood. "Toran, Ginnie … have you met Mrs. Owens?" He motioned them closer. "Marsha, this is my grandnephew, Toran, and my grandniece, Ginnie."

Toran reached his hand out and shook Mrs. Owens'. "It's nice to meet you."

Mrs. Owens smiled weakly. "It's nice to meet a friend of Pierce's."

"He's not my friend," Pierce snapped.

Ginnie dropped her hand when Mrs. Owens turned to Pierce. She and Toran exchanged panicked looks.

Toran took a breath in and exhaled slowly before replying in a calm voice. "I'd *like* to be your friend."

"We're not going to be buddy-buddy just because your dad's making you be nice to me. We still have some things to settle." Pierce spat the words and turned away.

Anger boiled in Ginnie, her good intentions rapidly washing away while promptly being replaced with the desire to stand up for her brother.

Dad gave her a warning shake of his head and faced Pierce. "It was Toran's idea to come. I told him he didn't have to. Toran and Ginnie just want to help. They'd like to be your friends."

"Like I'd be friends *with her*."

Pierce's glare sent a shudder through her. Ginnie thought briefly of a movie she'd seen where the villain could turn people into a pile of dust. *I'd be a molehill in one-point-six seconds flat.*

Just as she opened her mouth to respond with equal malice, her eyes lit on Pierce's multi-colored face. His swelling cheek transported her memory to a time when such a bruise had been imprinted on six-year-old Tillie's cheek … also the result of the angry swing of a man's hand.

The ugly retort melted in her throat, her initial impulse to one-up Pierce disappearing as quickly as her best friend's face had materialized.

CHAPTER FORTY-SIX:
THE REVELATION

Ginnie blinked. Pierce's multi-colored face, complete with scowl, reappeared. A jumble of feelings ran over one another: anger, loathing, disgust … sorrow. At Pierce … because of Pierce … *for* Pierce.

Her gaze locked with Pierce's. Ginnie recognized a look of Tillie's that she often pushed to the back of her mind, its presence much too painful to acknowledge.

Ginnie couldn't describe it and she didn't want to. She just needed to make it go away. Snatches of recent conversations whispered loudly in her mind. *You didn't do it yourself … apologize … needs a friend … save face.*

Her mouth opened and unrehearsed words rushed out. "Pierce, it's okay to be mad at me. I'm sorry about the fight at school and the movies. I just got lucky. I'd like to be your friend, but it's okay if you don't want to be mine."

Pierce's mouth opened, then closed … then opened. "I don't want to be your friend." He lurched forward, pointing an angry finger at her. "This is all your fault."

Ginnie willed her body to freeze. "I know."

Dad moved between them. "Whoa. Say what you need to, but do it from over there. We didn't come here to fight."

"I need to get even, that's what I need."

"Even for what?" Toran stepped in front of Dad. "Because she didn't give you that black eye, *I* did."

Pierce snorted. "No, *you* didn't. *You* couldn't hurt a flea." Pierce whirled from them.

Toran didn't black Pierce's eye? Then who did?

Ginnie and Toran exchanged the unspoken questions and then answered them as clearly as if the answer had been projected on a movie screen. *His father.*

CHAPTER FORTY-SEVEN: TORAN'S TURN

Both relief and disappointment that he wasn't the cause of Pierce's multi-colored eye swirled inside Toran. It really bugged him that Pierce had contempt for his fighting ability, especially since Ginnie had shown them both up.

Toran took another peek at Pierce's messed up face and resolved to let his own frustrations go.

Pierce had enough to worry about and violence wasn't Toran's style anyway. He hated it when Ginnie just bickered with him.

He actually reveled in the power to make Ginnie absolutely crazy at times by being kind and sensible when she exploded. And it didn't hurt that it kept him out of trouble with their dad, either. Toran liked life better when he was in control of his free time.

But how was he going to show Pierce he wanted to be friends? Pierce hated his guts. He wasn't buying Ginnie's apology. But maybe Pierce would be more receptive to one from him, man-to-man.

"I'm glad I didn't black your eye, Pierce. It looks like it really hurts. And I *do* want to be your friend." He glanced from Pierce then around the room, trying to figure out what he could say to get Pierce to lighten up. Then it hit him. "Maybe you'd like to come out to the farm and check out our animals? My cat just had kittens and one of our hogs had eleven piglets. We have to feed the runt with a baby bottle. It's kinda fun. Maybe you'd like to try?"

Pierce's snarl turned into an apprehensive line, then almost a soft smile. "Do baby hogs bite?"

"No, but it tickles if you let it suck your finger."

"That sounds kinda cool." Pierce turned to his mom. "Could we go see the animals?"

She nodded.

Pierce eyed Ginnie, then turned to Toran. "How many horses you got?"

"I don't have any, but Ginnie has one. Austin and Pete Jr. each have one. I bet we could borrow theirs, don't you think, Dad?"

"I'll bet the Chandlers would agree," Dad said.

"What about a B-B-Q if he comes over?" Ginnie asked.

Uncle Ben smiled. "I was just going to suggest that. We have a freezer full of new beef. Steaks and burgers are best on the grill. Would you like that, Pierce?"

Pierce looked like he'd died and gone to heaven. "Steaks? For real?"

"Even better … they're Uncle Ben's steaks. He makes the best," Ginnie added.

Toran could tell she hoped to win him over. He could also tell that Pierce wasn't going to make it easy for her. The bigger boy all but ignored her, focusing on Uncle Ben. "What are you making with the steaks?"

"Pierce," Mrs. Owens scolded.

Uncle Ben just smiled. "What would you like? Baked potatoes? Baked beans? Vi here makes the best potato salad."

"That's high praise, Dad." Vi pushed her auburn waves behind her ear and smiled at Pierce. "My dad is the best cook this side of the Mississippi. You're in for a treat."

Pierce turned to Uncle Ben. "You cook? That's women's work. Grilling's one thing, but potato salad?" His tone dripped with disappointment.

Toran held back a laugh when Dad pointed to the door for Ginnie's sake. Her mouth closed in mid-protest, without uttering a word. *Man, I wish I could figure out how to get her to keep quiet. My life would be so much easier.*

Vi didn't look too happy about Pierce's comment, but had the sense to not say anything. She pasted on a pleasant smile and sent Ginnie a sympathetic look.

Ginnie smirked and rolled her eyes.

"Pierce, would you agree that one of the true pleasures in life is a well cooked meal?" Uncle Ben asked.

"Well, *yeah*."

Uncle Ben took in Pierce's doubtful look, then scanned the rest of the family. "I'd like to make a deal with you. If you'll agree to give Ginnie and Toran a chance to make amends, I'll cook you a feast you won't ever forget. And if you like what I make, I'll have you over another day and teach you how to cook it, deal?"

Pierce eyed Ginnie suspiciously. "How much steak can I have?"

Uncle Ben chuckled. "As much as you want."

"My Uncle Jake makes the best homemade ice cream," Ginnie added, still trying to win Pierce over.

Toran wasn't about to be outdone. "Have you ever had strawberries picked fresh from the vine? Some of our plants are blooming a little early. I'm sure Uncle Ben wouldn't mind us picking some to eat and adding them to the ice cream."

"I wouldn't mind at all," Uncle Ben agreed. "Then I'd have a good reason to make my mama's strawberry bread." He winked at Pierce. "You haven't really lived until you've tried Oma West's strawberry bread."

"Strawberry bread sounds weird, but I like strawberries," Pierce said.

"Don't worry, Pierce. I don't think Uncle Ben knows how to cook anything bad," Toran assured him.

"Except fish. *Ick*." Ginnie rolled her eyes, adding quickly, "But everything *else* is yummy."

Mrs. Owens smiled. "I remember you brought some delicious chocolate chip cookies for our class one Sunday."

"Vi made some yesterday." He took Mrs. Owens' hand in his. "So it's settled. You come out to the farm tomorrow for a visit. Things'll look better then."

For the first time all night, the room filled with a peaceful feeling. The nice feeling lasted for just as long as it took for two uniformed police officers to rap loudly on the front door.

CHAPTER FORTY-EIGHT:
OFFICER MALLEY

Ginnie followed Dad and Toran outside to speak with one of the officers, while the other stayed inside. She was embarrassed to admit to why they had come to Pierce's in the first place.

"Just tell the truth," Dad said.

She and Toran tripped over each other explaining the original fight at school, the fight at the movies, Pierce twisting Ginnie's wrist, and their plan for revenge.

"Maybe you two should stay away from Pierce from now on," Officer Malley suggested.

"Since he's coming out to our house tomorrow, that might be kinda hard," Ginnie replied.

Officer Malley twisted quickly to Dad. "You really think that's a good idea?"

"They will be well supervised." Dad stood straighter, like he was daring the officer to disagree. "If they can come to some understandings outside of school, they can help Pierce. It's not going to be easy for him to show up at school on Monday morning looking like that."

The lead ball returned to Ginnie's middle.

School wouldn't be easy for any of them. Maybe Dad would write them an excuse and let them ditch.

One glance to her male parental unit squashed that idea. *Nah, probably not.*

"I hope you're right." The officer closed his notebook and studied

Toran's face, then Ginnie's. "Are you two up for that? I'd hate to have to break up a fight at school."

"Yes, sir. I don't even care if he doesn't want to be my friend. I'm not going to let anyone tease Pierce," Ginnie insisted, glancing at Dad for approval.

"Just keep your hands to yourself if someone does."

Dad gave her shoulder a gentle squeeze and smiled at the officer. "Being a good friend to her brother and sister is what got her into this mess. She's nothing if not loyal to those she cares about."

Sister? Oh … Tillie. Yeah.

A huge grin started on her lips and spread its warmth all through her insides, lightening the lead ball.

CHAPTER FORTY-NINE:
AN APOLOGY ... OF SORTS

After changing into her pajamas, Ginnie knocked on her brother's door from her room and waited for him to open it. Toran motioned her to enter his room. "Are you really going to be okay with Pierce coming to the farm tomorrow?"

Ginnie shrugged. "Sure, why not?"

"Because I don't think Pierce likes you at all ... and you have a pretty quick temper. Smarting off to him's not gonna go over well."

"I can be just as calm as you."

Toran snorted his disagreement.

Ginnie buffed her fingers against her green top. "I did good tonight, even though he has some pretty lame opinions about girls."

"Yeah, but only because Dad was standing there. Dad won't be there on Monday."

"I can be there if I need to be," Dad said, breezing in Toran's other door. He locked his eyes on Toran's. "Do I need to be?"

Ginnie dimmed her grin. Being cocky would cost her all the bonus points she'd just earned. And she liked Dad's attention being more focused on Toran than herself.

Dad pointed to Toran's bed. "I need to clear up something with both of you. Have a seat."

"Are we in trouble?" Ginnie asked.

"A little, but I owe you both an apology as well. Sit down and I'll make it quick." An apology was certainly better than a punishment. Intrigued,

Ginnie followed Toran to his bed.

Dad pulled out the shiny black desk chair Toran used for his schoolwork, flipped it around and straddled it, facing each of them. He took a second to gather his thoughts. "I'm not sure how to start."

Toran rubbed a palm down his red pajama pants. "Take your time, we'll wait."

Dad smiled. "Thanks." He glanced around the room for a few seconds before focusing on Ginnie. "You've put me on an emotional roller coaster these last couple days and I'm really not sure what to do about it."

Great, everything's my fault again. So much for an apology. Ginnie stiffened. *So what color am I gonna be painting the fence?*

Dad squeezed her knee firmly. "I haven't been so mad, glad, proud, disappointed, worried, and scared all at once—*because of you*—in a while." He winked. "Don't do that again for a good long time. I need a little time to regroup."

Proud? Of what?

Toran chuckled when Ginnie sent him a 'what's-he-talking-about?' look. She turned back to their dad, completely lost. "So am I in trouble or not?"

"Yes … and no," Dad replied.

"Thanks for clearing that up." She fought the urge to roll her eyes. It occurred to her that as long as he's sitting on the fence, it might be better not to push him into the pasture with a charging bull.

Maybe humor would help. "Can you just tell me what color you want the fence painted? Blue might be nice, though emerald green is my favorite color. It'd sorta blend in with the cornstalks, doncha think?"

Dad leaned forward and laughed. "We'll leave fence painting to school suspensions or something more serious."

"Oka-a-a-y. So I'm not in *serious* trouble?"

"No, not serious trouble." He brushed her cheek gently with his thumb. "But I owe you an apology for not handling your fight with Pierce better—either of them. After tonight, I realize that I should have come at this whole thing differently. I'm sorry for not being more understanding … or approachable. Can you forgive me?"

Huh? "Are you joking or for real? 'Cause I can't tell."

"For real. I messed up." He ducked his head a little. "I've been so frustrated with you because of your stubbornness and sneaking that I completely missed that I should have figured out *why* you were sneaking."

Since she still didn't have a clue as to what he was apologizing for, Ginnie kept quiet. Maybe some of his ramblings would eventually make sense.

"I've always tried to be open to you, but I must not be doing a good job because you finished painting the fence one night and got into a fight the next." He motioned toward the lane. "I grounded you this afternoon and you go sneaking off to pull a prank a couple hours later." He sat straighter and eyed each of them closely. "What part of my telling you that I didn't like you deceiving me made you decide to sneak over to Pierce's and prank him?"

Ginnie shrugged. "None of it."

"Then why did you?" Dad asked.

Ginnie held up her arm. "We pranked him because he hurt my wrist. It didn't have anything to do with you."

"What she *means*," Toran added, frowning at her. "Is that those are two separate issues."

"Really?" Dad questioned, his tone incredulous. "Because in my mind, they go hand-in-hand. Please enlighten me."

"*You* didn't hurt my arm, *Pierce* did. So I wanted to pay him back." *What's so hard about that?*

"He threatened Ginnie. I'm her brother." Toran slid forward. "I'm supposed to look out for her, right? Just like Uncle Jake said about you tonight."

"Hey! I'm not helpless," Ginnie protested.

"That's apples and oranges." Dad ignored Ginnie and shook his head at Toran, looking like he was lost in an episode of the Twilight Zone. "Jake's a hot head and I can't stop him from doing stupid things." He wagged a scolding finger between Ginnie and Toran. "You two, on the other hand, are a different story. I'd like to think I have some kind of influence over what *you* do."

Toran scooted back on the bed a little. "Dad, I get that we shouldn't have done it, but really, Ginnie would have gone without me. So I went with her. That's better than her going off by herself, right?"

"Are you kidding me?" Dad stood quickly, nearly knocking over the chair. "It never even occurred to you to tell *me* that Pierce hurt her? You're her brother, *but I'm her dad*. Since when have I ever let anyone hurt either of you and get away with it?"

He didn't wait for an answer. Dad crossed the room, pacing

between both doors several times, shaking his head and muttering under his breath.

Ginnie had the feeling that Dad would be buying more paint if they couldn't figure out what he wanted to hear.

So much for an apology.

Toran's eyes widened. "Dad, I thought you'd want me to go with her and keep her out of trouble."

Dad crossed the room in three steps, frustration coloring his face. "And just how well did that plan work out? You two committed a misdemeanor, cops were involved, Ray got arrested, our whole family—"

"—helped Pierce and his mom ..." Ginnie finished, sliding to her feet. "Isn't *that* part okay?"

"Of course, but—" Dad reached an arm around each of their shoulders. "You are too much like your mom." He kissed the top of Ginnie's head and whispered. "She didn't play fair either. What am I going to do with you?"

CHAPTER FIFTY:
THE TWILIGHT ZONE

Forgive me?" Ginnie suggested, feeling like Dad had pulled her along into his own personal episode of the Twilight Zone.

"My intention was to apologize to you and ask *your* forgiveness, not the other way around. How'd we end up here in Crazy Town?"

Ginnie giggled. "Through a wormhole?"

Dad chuckled. "That's as good an explanation as anything I'm coming up with." He motioned them to Toran's bed and straddled his chair again. "I just wanted to say I was sorry for punishing you guys without finding out *why* you felt like you couldn't trust me with the truth."

"We trust you," Ginnie protested.

Dad lowered his voice. "Apparently you didn't. You got into a fight at the movies and hid it from me." He put up a hand to stop any more protests. "I'm not blaming you. Tillie told me you didn't want to paint the fence again and then, when I saw Pierce's face tonight, I realized that *I* was part of the problem."

Ginnie looked at Toran to see if he was making sense of Dad's apology. Her brother seemed confused as well.

"You shouldn't have to worry about being punished when a bully is bothering you. You should feel safe coming to me with any problem. I let you down. For that, I am sorry."

For once, Ginnie didn't know what to say. Or blurt without thinking. While she processed Dad's words, Toran let out a long breath. "We know that, Dad. You listened tonight when we needed you to help Pierce."

"But I should have handled the first fight differently. Pierce targeted both of you ... and Toran, no offense, but I owe Ginnie an apology. She stood up for you and I punished her for it. I was wrong to do that."

Ginnie snapped her eyes to Dad's. "Really?"

He nodded. "I took Toran's side because in the past, when all else was equal, you've been impulsive and overbearing and *truthfully* … you've been wrong."

Ginnie scrunched her face in disgust. "That's a pretty lame apology." She turned from them both.

"Let me finish. You were right to stand up for Toran."

"No, she wasn't!"

Ginnie swiveled back, willing to listen. "Go on …"

Dad smiled. "While I *still* believe you should have let Toran handle Pierce and I believe your brother *could* have managed very well without you—that doesn't change the fact that Pierce is twice as big as you. You reacted the way you always have, to protect him. Something I've always encouraged you to do."

"But I didn't *need* protecting." Toran pounded a fist on his comforter. "She made things worse."

"I know, but she did it for the right reasons."

Toran planted his feet on the floor and stood quickly. "She embarrassed me."

"I know that, *too*. But if she were your twin *brother* instead of your sister, would you be embarrassed?"

"Probably not as much …"

"Exactly." Dad motioned him to sit. "If your mom were here, you'd both be in a martial arts class, learning how to defend yourselves as well as learning to control certain impulsive tendencies." He eyeballed Toran, then let his gaze linger on Ginnie. "Which is something I should look into."

Toran grinned. "Cool."

Ginnie groaned.

"At any rate, I made the presumption that Ginnie nailed a kid pretty much her size, probably because you two, give or take a couple inches here and there are roughly the same size. Not that fighting with *anyone* is appropriate. You know *that*, right?"

Ginnie nodded.

"The truth is—and you can take this as a compliment as well as an excuse if you'd like Gin—by all counts you knocked him down pretty quickly at school, so I guess I didn't consider that you were in any real danger."

Not sure how that made her feel, Ginnie clamped her jaw shut, slid her hands under her thighs, determined to hear him out.

"Then I saw Pierce go for you tonight and I realized that not only is he a big, angry guy, he didn't care that I stood between the two of you. Since I have a good ten inches on him and I'm an adult who also happens to be your dad, he should have had more self-control … *and he didn't.*"

Dad stood, pushed the chair back and paced the length of the room, his lips forming words that he didn't speak.

He finally squatted in front of Ginnie and met her at eye level. "I realized how wrong I was to expect you to just reason with him. He worried *me* a little and I'm pretty sure I can take him if I needed to." A small smile lit on his lips. "But I'm getting my apology sidetracked again. Sorry."

"It's okay."

"No, Ginnie, it's not." He squeezed her knee emphatically. "And it's *not* your fault his dad got arrested, either. Ray lost control and treated Pierce horribly. You made that stop, but the reality is; he's probably going to blame you because it's easier than blaming his father."

Dad stood, then sat on the bed between them and pulled each close, resting his chin on the crown of Ginnie's head. "This is so crazy. You were wrong to prank him, but by doing so ... you helped a kid who really needed help." He squeezed her tight and chuckled. "Things were s-o-o-o much easier when you guys were three. You didn't have a problem I couldn't solve. Right was right, wrong was wrong, and giving you a juice box or a nap made everything better."

Ginnie grinned. "I could go for a chocolate malt ..."

"So you think the going rate for parental guilt should be chocolate malts?" Dad teased.

Toran smiled. "Works for me."

"Me too." Dad stood. "Fine. Chocolate malts it is, as long as you promise ..." He raised his pointer finger. "One, I want to know if anybody threatens you." He raised a second finger. "Two, I want to know everything going on in all aspects of your lives and most of all ..." He raised a third finger. "Three, I want you to know that I am here for you, each of you... forever and always. Deal?"

Ginnie and Toran made a show of passing looks back and forth, arching their eyebrows, and rubbing their chins until each of them burst out laughing.

"Deal."

CHAPTER FIFTY-ONE:
CRAZY TOWN

Tillie's heart raced when she heard three quick knocks on her door. It squeaked open to reveal Mom, standing with an odd smile on her face.

"Mom, you scared me."

"Sorry. Todd's here. He wants to take us out for ice cream. Do you want to go?"

D.T's here? Uh yeah, I wanna go.

"Of course. Just a minute." Tillie threw off her covers and snatched up a pair of jeans. "What time is it?"

"Ten-fifteen. Oh, no need to change." Mom peeked in Tillie's mirror and ran her fingers through her auburn waves. "Apparently it's a pajama party. We're going through the drive-thru."

"Awesome sauce. What's the occasion?"

Mom shrugged. "Just because."

Tillie followed Mom out to D.T's car, and slid in next to Ginnie, giggling. They bumped fists and squealed.

Toran shook his head and smiled. "Girls."

D.T. winked at Tillie, then wiggled his eyebrows playfully at Mom. "True. Can't live with'em. Can't live without'em." He adjusted the rearview mirror. "Get used to it, son, because that's the truth. And trust me; it's more fun with'em than without'em."

Ginnie cupped her hand around Tillie's ear. "Dad's a little crazy tonight, but go with it. We're getting chocolate malts."

"Yum, why are we getting malts?"

"'Cause Dad feels bad about busting us for getting in a fight with

Pierce."

"Why? We shoulda told him."

Ginnie shrugged. "I think he feels bad about Pierce's dad getting arrested."

"Got arrested?" Tillie jerked backwards. "For what?"

"For beating up Pierce."

She sucked in a horrified breath. "Was Pierce hurt bad?"

"His dad didn't break anything, but his face is pretty messed up."

Tillie slumped forward, catching her face in her hands. She planted her elbows on her knees and willed herself to take a breath. Her arms shook as unexplained panic took over, squeezing the air out of her lungs.

Ginnie shook her arm. "Are you okay?"

Her head slid slowly side to side, her chest tightening like it was trapped in a vise, unable to let her lungs expand fully for a well needed breath. Fuzzy white noise buzzed in her head. She closed her eyes and tried not to let the all-too-familiar anxiety consume her.

CHAPTER FIFTY-TWO:
TOO MUCH REALITY

Tillie's bad reaction to the news that Pierce had been hurt, and his dad arrested, haunted Ginnie much of the night.

She distracted her friend the best she could while they were together.

Tillie finally relaxed enough to enjoy the ice cream.

But later in bed, Ginnie thought about Pierce and wondered if he reacted like Tillie when he thought of *his* father. Just thinking about Mr. Owens made her shudder. Living with him must seriously freak Pierce out.

It was one thing to think of Pierce as angry and mean, but picturing him as a scared kid like Tillie, brought a whole new way of thinking to consider.

Tillie was like a defenseless baby kitten. Everyone wanted to scoop her up and make her feel safe. Pierce was more like a prickly porcupine or a skunk who shouldn't be treated badly, but no one wanted to cuddle with either.

Now, Ginnie stood next to Calliope in their pasture, enjoying the last of the cool morning air before the humidity descended and made it hot.

Dad held the reins of Pete Jr.'s horse while Toran explained the mechanics of mounting Austin's black gelding, Traxx, to Pierce.

"Why's he got a dumb name like Traxx?"

"Cause his daddy came from the wrong side of the tracks," Ginnie answered, smiling.

Pierce creased his brow. "What's that supposed to mean?"

Toran chuckled. "His mom was a purebred race horse, but his daddy was a friendly sort from the neighboring farm. She jumped the fence one day and did a little sightseeing. His real name is Wrong Side of the Traxx. Austin just calls him Traxx though."

"Seriously?" Pierce cracked a smile.

"Yep. He's Calliope's best friend." Ginnie put her left foot in the stirrup. "Like this." She swung into the saddle in a single fluid motion. "Now *you* try."

"Easy cheesy." Pierce put his left foot in the stirrup, but unbalanced before he could get his right leg completely over the saddle. He grabbed onto the saddle horn as he fell.

In two strides, Dad reached for Pierce to keep him from landing on his rear and threw warning looks at Toran and Ginnie. They wiped the grins off their faces before Pierce could lift his head.

"It takes a couple tries sometimes. Put your foot in the stirrup, hold the saddle horn with your left hand and grab the other side of the saddle as you swing." Toran instructed quickly, before Pierce could utter a word.

A satisfactory grin soon replaced the automatic scowl on Pierce's face when he found himself sitting astride Traxx, clutching the saddle horn with both hands. "I did it."

Ginnie let out a relieved breath she didn't know she held. Normally she wouldn't think getting into a saddle was a big deal, but seeing the satisfaction on Pierce's face made her feel like a protective mother hen.

Toran beamed at him. "You sure did." He lifted Traxx's reins over the horse's head and placed them in Pierce's hands. "Don't pull on them hard. A gentle tug is all you need. How are you feeling?"

"Good. Can I ride him now?" Pierce kicked Traxx hard without waiting for an answer.

Ginnie turned Calliope to head off Traxx.

"Whoa!" Toran grabbed the bridle with one hand and stroked Traxx's neck with the other.

Toran put his hand up to shield his eyes from the sun. "*Gently* touch his sides with your heel. Otherwise, you'll hurt and confuse him. He's used to Austin. Hang on while I get on Ranger and then we can all ride together."

Dad went over the rules again with Pierce while Toran mounted Ranger. "Are you ready?"

"Of course. I came over here to ride, didn't I?"

Dad took in a sharp breath. "Traxx has feelings, just like you do. I know you're excited, but settle down a minute and you can go."

Ginnie waited for Pierce to explode.

Instead, he gave a conceding nod.

Wow, Dad's almost as good with Pierce as Uncle Ben.

Once Toran and Ranger flanked Pierce's other side, Dad let them go.

Pierce kicked Traxx a little too hard and jerked backward, grabbing the saddle horn. "Hey!"

"The reins Pierce, not the saddle horn," Toran called.

Pierce bobbed up and down like an apple in a bucket of water at a Halloween party. He clutched at the saddle horn as he fumbled for the reins.

Ginnie held her amused smile in check, but enjoyed Pierce's beaming grin. It didn't seem to matter to him that he could have a better ride. He seemed happy just to be on the horse at all.

She recalled her first ride on Calliope and relished the bubbling fizzy feeling of exhilaration. Ginnie kept Calliope in step with Traxx. "Relax and enjoy the ride. Let your body move to his rhythm. If you fight him, you'll be sore and it won't be as much fun."

Pierce nodded. "O-o-o-ka-a-a-a-y" His voice bobbed up and down with his body.

They neared the end of the pasture. "Pull his left rein just a little. He'll turn." She turned Calliope and waited for Pierce to do the same.

Toran came up on his other side. "You're doing great, Pierce."

Pierce grinned and kicked Traxx harder. He pulled ahead and the race was on.

Toran kept Ranger in step with Traxx. "Slow down as you get to the big tree."

Pierce frowned, but slowed Traxx when they got to a huge red maple. "Can we jump stuff? Like a fence?"

"No." Ginnie shook her head as she lined Calliope up on Traxx's other side. "Our mom died when her horse threw her. Dad won't let us do tricks."

A strange look crossed Pierce's face as her words sunk in. "Wow. That's rough."

Toran nodded. "But it's better than not being able to ride at all. Come on."

Ginnie and Pierce followed Toran to the front of the pasture where Dad leaned against the fence. Toran stopped Ranger and pointed to the gate. "Dad, can we go to the cut alfalfa field?"

Dad looked each of them over. "How are you feeling, Pierce?"

"Great. I can do this all day."

"Well, you probably don't want to. Tomorrow you'll be sore." Dad stroked Ranger and smiled. "Lunch is about done. Why don't you guys go around the cut field a couple times and then come back. You're looking good out there, Pierce."

"Thanks." Pierce's pleasant tone surprised Ginnie. For once he sounded like a regular kid.

"Safety first, but have fun."

And Dad sounds like Dad.

Ginnie laughed. "Yes, sir."

Toran led the way to the field. They lined up and raced. Pierce kicked Traxx harder and pulled into the lead.

Ranger caught up quickly.

Toran shook his head at Ginnie when Calliope gained on them. Ginnie scowled, but slowed her horse.

Ranger and Traxx raced neck and neck to the end.

"I thought you said your nag was a racehorse?" Pierce taunted.

So much for Pierce being nice. Ginnie forced a smile. "She's just being polite."

Toran turned Ranger. "Pierce, want to go again?"

Pierce nodded. "That was fun."

They raced up and down twice more. When he 'won,' Pierce grinned from ear to ear.

"Let's walk the horses cool and then water them," Toran said.

Pierce fidgeted in his saddle. "Let's go faster."

Toran shook his head. "We have to let them cool or they might founder. That's a bad thing."

Pierce grumbled under his breath, but nodded.

In a few minutes, they reached the farmhouse.

"Hey look, it's Tillie and Miss Amanda!" Ginnie squealed, waving at their friend as Tillie got out of her mom's car.

Tillie returned the wave as they rode past.

The smells from the B-B-Q grill on the sidewalk near the farmhouse made Ginnie's belly growl in anticipation.

Uncle Ben stood with a plate and Uncle Jake held a long fork and knife, checking and flipping steaks.

A table next to the porch held a bowl of potato salad and a bowl of 'green stuff'—the family's nickname for a delightful mixture of pineapple chunks, marshmallows, whipped topping and pistachio pudding.

Lunch would be ready soon.

"Be right back, Til," Ginnie called. She reached the pasture first, dismounted to open the gate and let the boys through. After unbuckling Calliope's saddle, she set it on the fence post. She wiped Calliope's sweaty back with a towel and led Calliope to the water trough.

Toran swung down from the saddle and waited for Pierce to do the same. Pierce used the stirrup as a step, but swung too quickly. He lost his balance, landing in an ungraceful squat. His familiar snarl was glued once again to his face when he stood.

"You did good Pierce. The first time I dismounted, I ended up on my rear." Toran gave him a hesitant smile. "At least *you* landed on your feet."

Ginnie hoped it would smooth Pierce's mood.

Pierce glanced around suspiciously, then returned Toran's smile. "Can we ride again?"

"After lunch. Want to see the kittens?" Toran offered.

Pierce nodded.

They took care of their horses and then made their way to the main barn.

Ginnie went the opposite way to catch up to Tillie.

CHAPTER FIFTY-THREE:
HAMILTON

After seeing Ginnie, Toran, and Pierce ride by her on the horses like they were old friends made Tillie feel better and worse about Pierce being at the farm. She'd felt so bad for Pierce last night when Ginnie explained about their prank going wrong, calling 9-1-1, and seeing Mr. Owens being driven off to jail.

She could imagine how frightened Pierce must have been. With the shade of the giant maple trees casting a shadow, his bruised face didn't look as glaring, but still sore. Pierce didn't seem to be in pain though. He actually seemed to be enjoying hanging out with Ginnie and Toran.

That's good.

When the three of them rounded the corner of the farmhouse to pasture the horses, Mom turned to her. "Don't stare, Tils. Just relax and you'll be fine."

"I am relaxed." But she wasn't, her heart thumped loudly in her chest. *Mom must be able to hear it.*

The front screen door squeaked open and D.T. came through. He saw them and hurried down the stairs. He winked at Tillie, and then drew Mom into a hug. "Mmm. Your perfume smells wonderful."

"Not as good as the steaks. Yum. I skipped breakfast so I would have plenty of room." Mom turned to Tillie. "Why don't you go find Ginnie and the boys?"

If she were Ginnie, Tillie would have teased Mom about wanting time alone with D.T. But since she wasn't, she decided to give them alone time anyway. She didn't want to embarrass them. She just wanted them to get with the program. The more opportunity they had to fall in love and realize it, the sooner they could get married and she and Mom could move in. "Sure. I'll help with the horses."

"Thanks Tillie." D.T.'s words sounded extra nice.

When she hurried toward the grill, D.T. kissed Mom extra-long. *Yes!*

Uncle Ben reached an arm to her.

Uncle Jake flipped a steak. "Hey, Turtle."

"Hey. Is Hamilton still on the bottle?"

Uncle Ben enveloped her in a hug. "For a couple more days. Why don't you mix the bottle and offer to let Pierce help you feed him? I'll bet he'd like that."

"Sure, Uncle Ben."

He gave her another squeeze and then let go.

"See ya!" Tillie hurried around the corner of the house. She waved to Ginnie, who had just closed the pasture gate, and motioned her to come. Tillie opened the side porch door and waited for Ginnie to go through.

They stopped by the box to check on Hamilton. He was the smallest in a litter of eleven baby hogs and was being bottle-fed by hand until he got bigger.

Tillie loved feeding him. She pretended he was a real baby. Toran named him Hamilton as a play on ham 'n' eggs. Tillie hoped they would never actually eat him, but reminded herself where bacon came from. *Maybe I'll become a vegetarian, but not til after lunch. Those steaks smell delicious.*

Hamilton pushed himself onto all fours and squealed his impatience for lunch.

Ginnie picked him up and followed Tillie to the kitchen.

CHAPTER FIFTY-FOUR: SISTERS

H I, girls. Did you come to help?" Vi asked when Tillie and Ginnie entered the kitchen.

"Sorta, Uncle Ben said I should make a bottle for Hamilton." Tillie smiled at Mrs. Owens, who sat at the counter slicing strawberries.

Tillie walked around her, stopping at the sink.

"You know where everything is. Make a four-ounce bottle. Hamilton is quite the piggy lately." Vi laughed at her joke and fished corn-on-the-cob out of boiling water into a deep bowl. "Gin, take him out to the porch please. I don't want him wetting in here."

"Sure, Vi."

"But let me see him first," Mrs. Owens said.

Ginnie stepped closer to Mrs. Owens, who 'oohed' and 'aahed' over the piglet, before she took Hamilton back to the porch.

"Marsha, have you met Tillie? She's been our family friend forever. Todd's dating her mom, so pretty soon Ginnie and I may each have a brand new sister."

"I thought Todd was your cousin?" Mrs. Owens asked, her face wrinkled in question.

Vi laughed. "Todd moved in when I was four and he was eleven, so he's always been more like a big brother. So that makes Amanda like my sister and Tillie will be Ginnie's. At any rate, they're already family."

Tillie felt a huge grin cross her face. A cool warmth flowed over her like a shadow from a shade tree, tingling her skin. "Hi."

She turned from Mrs. Owens, embarrassed at her joy, but not knowing why.

Tillie slid the baby hog formula and a bottle toward her, from the back of the counter. She filled the bottle halfway with warm water. After scooping the formula into the bottle, she screwed the lid on, and shook it over the sink.

"You're a regular farm girl, aren't you, Tillie?" Mrs. Owens asked.

"Almost."

Vi shook a corn-on-the-cob at her. "There's no 'almost' about it. Tillie's as much at home here as Ginnie. She pretty much lives here and we like it that way."

Tillie grinned bigger at Vi's scolding, feeling more like a West all the time. Ginnie sometimes complained about how bossy Vi was, but they both thought Vi was the best big sister, surrogate mom, and friend they could ask for.

Vi and Mom were good friends as well. At least once a month the four of them went out for a 'Girl's Night Out'.

I hope we still get to do that even after Vi gets married.

Vi's fiancé, Preston, proposed last week and ever since, Mom and Vi had been planning Vi and Preston's wedding.

Tillie was hoping Mom would take notes for her own wedding and that D.T. would hurry up and at least propose, even if he wasn't ready to set a date.

He asked Ginnie's mom to marry him soon after they met, so maybe Tillie wouldn't have to wait much longer.

The side porch screen door squeaked open and Hamilton squealed a duet with the door.

Time to feed the baby.

Tillie smiled at both women and hurried to the porch.

CHAPTER FIFTY-FIVE: PIERCE & HAMILTON

"W anna hold him, Pierce?" Ginnie asked while snuggling Hamilton.

"He's awfully little." Pierce scrunched his face, studying the baby pig.

"You won't break him. He's pretty sturdy." Ginnie lowered herself into a sitting position. "Oh, there's his bottle. Hi, Tillie. Pierce, can feed him, if you want to."

Pierce sat next to Ginnie and reached for the pig.

Hamilton squealed, causing Pierce to jerk backward.

Ginnie tried not to laugh.

Pierce was so much bigger than the tiny animal, but the boy seemed almost afraid of the runt. Pierce forced a smile, but still looked uncomfortable.

Then a miracle of sorts happened. Pierce wiggled his fingers at the pig and Hamilton stopped squealing. "It's okay, boy, I won't hurt you." The tenderness in Pierce's words made everyone look at him differently.

Tillie knelt next to him. "Here's his lunch."

Pierce lifted Hamilton onto his back like a human newborn to feed him.

The pig protested.

Toran turned him over. "Here, Pierce, like this." He set the runt on Pierce's lap and put the bottle in front of the pig.

Hamilton started sucking the plastic nipple.

"He would drink from his mom like this," Toran explained.

"That makes sense." Pierce took the bottle and laughed as Hamilton continued to gobble the milk. "Why isn't he with his mom?"

"She had eleven babies and couldn't feed them all. Hamilton couldn't keep up with all his brothers and sisters. And since he was the littlest, they shoved him aside," Toran explained.

"That's rough little fella, huh?" Pierce cooed.

Hamilton kept sucking on the bottle.

Tillie reached a hand to stroke the pig. "He's doing okay now. He gets lots of attention from us. In a few weeks, when he eats out of a bowl real well, he'll go back. He'll be big and strong and be able to keep up with the others."

Boots shuffled up the sidewalk.

Pierce tilted the bottle higher. "That's okay then. Maybe I can come out and feed him sometimes?"

"That would be great, Pierce. Huh, Uncle Ben?" Ginnie asked, spotting her great-uncle coming up the walk.

"Sounds fine to me. Pierce, you're a natural. We feed him every three to four hours at the moment. You should be able to get in at least one more feeding today if you like." Uncle Ben entered the side porch door. "Toran, why don't you stay with Pierce till Hamilton's had his lunch, then show Pierce where to wash up. Lunch is ready."

"Yes, sir," Toran answered.

Ginnie stood. "Tillie and I'll get cleaned up. Do you need help?"

"I think it's mostly ready. Vi might need some help. The Chandlers should be here any minute. Then we'll eat."

"Who're the Chandlers?" Pierce asked.

"Austin's family. We rode their horses earlier. So Uncle Ben invited them to lunch," Toran explained.

Pierce jerked his head toward Uncle Ben.

Uncle Ben squatted next to him. "Don't worry, Pierce. The Chandlers are good people. Austin wants to be your friend. I figure you can't have too many good friends and I've known the Chandlers since their grandpa and I were boys. Austin's dad and uncle were my boys' best friends. And Austin and Pete Jr. are good friends with Toran, Ginnie, and Tillie here. They're the 'Four Musketeers'. Maybe you'll be the fifth."

Pierce cast a suspicious look around the porch. "I don't know about that."

Uncle Ben stood. "You guys don't have to decide today. But you seem pretty at home here. We like having you, Pierce. That's the truth. Hamilton trusts you and animals are a pretty good judge of character."

"That's true, Pierce." Toran agreed, pointing to the pig, which lay on Pierce's lap napping as he finished his lunch. "He seems pretty content."

Pierce looked down and smiled at the sleeping pig.

.

CHAPTER FIFTY-SIX:
THE B-B-Q

Ginnie and Tillie each carried a bowl of food to the table in the front yard. The table overflowed with steaks, green beans, corn-on-the-cob, salad with assorted dressings, baked potatoes, butter, cheese, sour cream, and bacon.

Steam curled off the apple pies and the soft whirr of two ice cream makers swirling strawberry and French vanilla could be heard on the front porch.

Pierce's jaw dropped when his eyes took in the feast. He glanced down the lane and pointed at a blue minivan. "Is that the Chandler's?"

Dad followed his finger. "It sure is. You know Austin. Uncle Ben invited them to lunch when they dropped off the horses this morning."

Pierce grimaced and then took a breath. He let it out and looked at Uncle Ben.

"I haven't steered you wrong yet, have I?" Uncle Ben gave his shoulder a gentle squeeze. "And I won't. The Chandlers are good people. Right now, you and your mom could use more of those in your life."

Dad smiled and hitched a thumb at Uncle Ben. "Pierce, you're our friend now. And Wests don't do friendships half-way. That's Uncle Ben's rule. You've met my uncle. Do you want to argue with him?"

Pierce cast a glance at Uncle Ben. Ginnie could tell he was considering Dad's words. It didn't surprise her when Pierce gave a slight shake of his head. *Nobody* argued with Uncle Ben, at least not for long. "I guess not." Pierce threw a wistful look at the overflowing table.

Uncle Ben smiled. "As soon as they join us, we'll have a quick blessing and serve lunch."

"Okay."

Austin burst out of the van, and then slowed when he saw Pierce's stare. "Hey ... Pierce." Austin turned to Uncle Ben. "Hi, Uncle Ben. The food looks awesome. Thanks for inviting us."

Uncle Ben smiled. "Pierce was just saying how much fun he had riding Traxx."

"Good, he's a great horse. Maybe you'd like to come over to my house some time?" Austin's tone didn't seem as sincere as his words.

Seconds of silence passed.

"Thank you, Austin." Mrs. Owens took a step forward. "Pierce would like that, wouldn't you?"

"Sure, I guess." Pierce glanced between Austin and Uncle Ben. "Why did he call you Uncle Ben? You're *his* uncle too?"

"Some friends are just like family." Uncle Ben winked at him. "Pete Sr. and his brother Luke always called me 'Uncle Ben' because my boys do. You can call me that too, if you like."

"I'll think about it." Pierce eyed the table again. "Can we eat now?"

Uncle Ben laughed as he nodded. "As soon as we bless the food."

When Austin's folks reached the rest of the group, the men took off their hats and Uncle Ben offered a quick blessing on the lunch, the hands that prepared it, and spent a minute asking that all the guests would feel welcome and enjoy the afternoon.

After the "Amens", Pierce hurried to the table. Dad suggested all the kids get their food and sit under the shade of the big maple near the brook.

Pierce heaped his plate full. Toran insisted Tillie go ahead of him. Ginnie and Austin took two corn-on-the-cobs each. Pete Jr. piled on the steak.

"Save room for the ice cream and pie," Uncle Jake suggested.

Tillie grinned. "Did you make the ice cream, Uncle Jake?"

"Of course. That's my specialty."

"Yum! I'm definitely *saving* room." Tillie put back a second piece of steak.

"I'll just *make* room," Pierce said, adding more bacon to his potato.

Uncle Jake chuckled. "You do that. You won't be disappointed."

The kids settled in the shade with their lunch. Dad brought over six cans of soda pop. "All good?" They mumbled their assurances while enjoying the feast.

"All right. Let the grownups get a chance to eat lunch and we'll see about dessert." He turned and left.

Ginnie was amazed at out how much food Pierce could put away. He rivaled Pete Jr., who at five years their senior, seemed to have a hollow leg.

She reached for her soda and ended up with a shirt full of food. "Oops. I better change."

"Or call Bandit and Reckless over. They'll lick you clean," Toran teased.

"No thanks. I got this." Ginnie jumped up and hurried inside to change her shirt. The phone rang as she started up the stairs. "I'll get it."

An automatic message stating there was a collect call from the county jail talked over her greeting.

"Who is it, Gin?" Dad asked.

Ginnie walked over to the screen door and looked out, avoiding Mrs. Owens' eyes. "It's Pierce's dad. Do I accept the call or not?"

CHAPTER FIFTY-SEVEN:
PHONE CALL

Uncle Ben offered Mrs. Owens a sympathetic smile and raised his brow in question.

Mrs. Owens nodded, scrunching her napkin.

Uncle Ben stood. "Ginnie, please accept the call." He walked towards the door.

Ginnie pushed the number one as instructed. "Where is my family and—" A shiver ran down her spine as filthy words spewed from the receiver. She nearly dropped it, the voice so spiteful that the phone seemed to bite.

Uncle Ben took the phone and put it behind his back. "Sorry, Gin. I'll take it from here."

Ginnie nodded and continued up the stairs.

"Ray, we're not going to get far if ..." Uncle Ben hurried into the study and closed the door.

Yikes! Dad'd be serving me a bar of soap if I talked like that. Poor, Pierce! Ginnie crossed Toran's room into hers and shut the door, shaking her head. *I'm glad our family doesn't talk like that.*

Just as she slid her T-shirt over her head, Tillie knocked on the door. "Come in."

Tillie hurried into her room. "Was that really Pierce's dad? What did he say?"

Ginnie shook her head. "You don't want to know. And I'm not allowed to repeat it."

Tillie giggled and then her voice turned sober. "Pierce took off.

Toran, Austin, and Pete Jr. ran after him."

Ginnie's eyes popped. "Where'd he go?"

"Just down the lane. He stopped running when they caught up to him. They were walking back when I left. I feel bad for Pierce." Tillie sighed and dropped her gaze to her sandals. "I know what it's like to have a father like that. You're really lucky that *your* dad's nice."

"Yeah, but I wish I had a mom. *Yours* is great." Ginnie walked over to her dresser, picked up her brush and pulled the elastic out of her hair.

"If they keep dating we'll *both* get two good parents." Tillie peeked in the mirror and ran her fingers through her hair, almost singing the words.

Ginnie nodded, then brushed her hair and re-braided it.

Each startled when they heard a loud knock on the door.

"Come in," Tillie and Ginnie called together.

Uncle Jake poked his head in. "Are you okay?"

Ginnie shrugged and turned back to her mirror. "Why wouldn't we be?"

"No reason. Tillie disappeared after your dad followed the boys." Uncle Jake winked at them. "Vi, Lauren, and Amanda are hovering over Marsha. I felt like a fifth wheel, with all the estrogen around. So I thought I'd check on you, being the awesome uncle I am and all."

"And humble." Ginnie reminded him and rolled her eyes. "Don't forget humble."

"Of course." He wiggled his eyebrows. "Want some ice cream? It's done."

"Sure." Tillie turned to him. "Uncle Jake?"

He grinned. "Turtle?"

"I know you and Jasper used to be friends. But he's just like Pierce's dad. How could you be friends with a person like that? *You're* not mean."

Her accusing tone sent his smile fleeing. He cleared his throat. "That was a long time ago." He hooked his thumb through his belt loop. "And believe it or not, he wasn't as bad as Pierce's dad."

Tillie's stare bore through him. "He's awful. What did you possibly see in him?"

"You know Tillie, I saw Jasper's face worse than Pierce's, more than once." He paused when Tillie's mouth dropped. "One time his eye was swollen shut for days. Jasper had it pretty bad. Child abuse wasn't really talked about then and people looked the other way. Agencies didn't get involved. Uncle Ben was the exception to the rule and tried to help him. Jasper's father let him … a time or two. But it was a different time."

Tillie paled as Ginnie sucked in a breath.

Uncle Jake's tone softened. "Tillie, I know he hurt you and that was wrong. But Jasper was no stranger to abuse." He unhooked his thumb and rubbed his palm on his jeans. "One time, his dad beat him with a phone cord. His back was beyond horrible … bruised and slashed. For once, Oscar Taylor knew he'd gone too far."

Ginnie swallowed hard enough to hear her ears pop.

Uncle Jake brushed loose strands of Tillie's hair out of her face. "Uncle Ben patched up his back and was so mad, sad, and frustrated that he went to the barn to chop wood. I popped out there to ask him something and found him with tears streaming down his cheeks. It was a bit unnerving." Uncle Jake let out a soft sigh. "The only other time I've seen Uncle Ben cry was when my folks died. Don't judge Jasper so harshly, Turtle. *His* dad wasn't a good example of how a dad should be."

Tillie crossed her arms and grimaced.

"*Most* of the time, he was a good dad to you. He always brought you over when I was home on leave. He used to tell me that you and your mom were the best things that ever happened to him. Most of the time he treated you guys pretty good."

"I *used* to love him." Tillie jutted out her chin. "But I don't anymore. I don't want him to come back—ever."

Uncle Jake took a step closer and offered each girl an arm, pulling them close. He kissed the top of Tillie's head and whispered. "You don't mean that."

Tillie shook her head. "You can't love someone and hurt them at the same time."

"Love's an amazing quality, but it's not always enough." Uncle Jake hugged Tillie closer. "You know … the truth is, Jasper left *because* he loved you. His dad made him feel like he wasn't worth the spit it took to shine his shoes. He felt that way the last time he hurt you."

"How do you know?"

The hurt in Tillie's voice caused a lump in Ginnie's throat. She could hardly swallow.

"Because he told me so." He shifted uncomfortably. "I tracked him to a bar after he hurt your mom the last time. I gave him a taste of what he dished out."

A tiny smile lit on Tillie's lips. "You hit him for me?"

Uncle Jake nodded. "But beating him up didn't make me feel as good as I thought it would. After a few punches he stopped hitting me back and just let me beat him. He told me he knew he was a snake." Uncle Jake wiped his hands on his jeans again. "I told him to man up or leave, but that he'd better keep his hands to himself. He stayed sober for a while and tried to change. Then he lost his job ..."

Seconds passed in silence.

Uncle Jake's eyes locked on Tillie's. "But he bolted before he could hurt you or Amanda again. He left a message on our answering machine asking us to look out for you. He said he was sorry he couldn't be the husband and father your mom and you deserved. He did keep his word to not hurt you guys again. That ought to count for something."

Tillie sighed. "I guess it should."

"Let it, Turtle. You'll feel better. And what'll make you feel *even better* is the scrump-dilly-umptious ice cream I made. Come on, Trouble, you too."

Ginnie giggled as he squeezed each of them into a hug. He walked them to the door and opened it. "Oh, and by the way..." He tossed each of them a mischievous grin.

Tillie planted a hand on her hip. "What?"

"You're it!" He tugged each girl's hair and scrambled down the stairs.

Ginnie dashed after him with Tillie close on her heels.

They burst through the screen door, barely missing Vi, and rushed down the concrete porch stairs to the grass.

Uncle Jake tripped over a rock and fell.

Ginnie threw herself on top of him, tickling his side. Tillie wasted no time tackling him as well.

Toran and Austin also piled on top of him.

"Help! Todd, get them off of me." Uncle Jake grabbed legs and tickled, but his attackers just laughed.

Dad ignored him and offered everyone ice cream instead. Austin and Toran got off of Uncle Jake.

Pierce rushed to Dad.

Uncle Jake tweaked Tillie's nose and sat up. "Oh, sure. Beat up a dude and then steal his ice cream. What a bunch of thugs."

Uncle Ben opened the screen door. "How's about a bowl of vanilla to go?" He stopped in front of Mrs. Owens. "Don't worry. I'll take care of things."

Vi gave Mrs. Owens a hug when Uncle Ben turned.

Pierce stood in Uncle Ben's path. "Are you going to get my dad out of jail?"

Uncle Ben rubbed Pierce's cheek with his thumb. "I'm not sure yet." His voice lowered. "Do you have a message for him?" Pierce nodded and crooked his finger.

Uncle Ben bent his ear to Pierce's mouth. "You have my word. I'll let him know."

Dad handed Uncle Ben a bowl of ice cream and a spoon. "Want some company?"

"No, thanks. Enjoy the day. Ray and I have a few things to settle."

CHAPTER FIFTY-EIGHT: DR. HAMILTON

After Uncle Ben left, Pierce looked at everybody, dashed down the steps, and around the corner.

D.T. shook his head at Toran and Ginnie, and then followed Pierce. Tillie swallowed hard and rushed after them, pleading. "Let me talk to him. I can help."

"He's too upset. I don't want you caught in his anger." D.T. pointed to the cars parked in front of the farmhouse. "I'll see to Pierce. You go back with the others."

Tillie stopped walking. Then she thought the better of things. "No, sir." She caught up to D.T. about the same time he spotted Pierce.

She peeked in the side porch screening.

Pierce sat next to Hamilton's box, holding the runt.

After opening the screen door, D.T. shook his head at Tillie and motioned again for her to leave.

Tillie licked her lips and stood her ground. "I can help."

They stared at each other for a few seconds before D.T. nodded for her to go ahead of him.

She sat next to Pierce.

D.T. stopped a few feet from them.

"What do *you* want?" Pierce growled, petting Hamilton a little too hard. The pig squealed.

It took every ounce of courage Tillie could muster to speak. "My birth father is like your dad. He used to hurt us before he left."

"You don't know what you're talking about." Pierce's words dripped with spite.

"Yes, I do." Tillie surprised herself with the confidence she felt as she continued to talk. "Jasper used to scream at my mom and me and blame us for stuff that wasn't our fault. He pushed us and hit us. He made my mom cry all the time. Until Uncle Ben and Uncle Jake made him leave."

Pierce did a double take. "How'd they do that? Make him leave, I mean?"

Tillie shrugged. "They talked to him and then he left."

"My dad's okay ... *most* of the time." Pierce grimaced at her, daring her to argue. "I don't want him to leave."

"I'm sure he won't then. But Uncle Ben has a way of making people *want* to behave." Tillie pushed her hair out of face and twirled a long whisp around her finger. "Maybe he can help your father be nicer."

"Well ... maybe. But he better not make my dad leave." Pierce pointed Hamilton at her, who squealed his protest. *"He loves us."*

"I'm sure he does." Tillie glanced at Pierce and repeated Uncle Jake's thoughts. "But sometimes love's not enough."

"It's enough." Pierce spat his words and cuddled Hamilton against his chest. "It *has* to be."

CHAPTER FIFTY-NINE: STATUE TAG

Uncle Jake stood in Ginnie's way when she tried to follow Tillie. "Your dad will watch out for her. How's about a game of Statue Tag? You can be 'It' first."

"That's lame. No one wants to be 'It' first," Ginnie complained, trying to go around him.

He matched her steps, blocking her every movement and gave her "the look" … something he seldom did.

Ginnie crossed her arms and debated whether she would stand up to him or not. She felt a light touch on her arm.

"Come with me, please."

Uncle Jake gave a quick nod as Ginnie put a name to the voice. *Miss Amanda.*

Casting a final glance at the corner of the farmhouse, Ginnie turned and let Miss Amanda lead her away.

"I just want to help," Ginnie said.

"You are, by letting Tillie and your dad talk to Pierce. They'll be fine. Let's play Statue Tag. I'll be 'It'."

Ginnie looked at Miss Amanda's feet.

She wore brand new white tennis shoes that matched her knee-length crisp white denim shorts. Her bright pink top was a classy t-shirt, not a regular 'T'. Everything about Miss Amanda was simple and beautiful. And her perfume smelled lovely, like Mama's.

"Okay. You wore the right shoes today," Ginnie teased, recalling last week's game where Miss Amanda wore sandals that broke soon after they started.

"I did. I want half-a-chance when I play against your sneaky Uncle Jake." Miss Amanda tossed her auburn waves in Uncle Jake's direction.

"Sneaky? I'm hurt. Is it my fault you didn't come prepared to play properly?" He wiggled his eyebrows playfully as he neared.

"Since I dressed for the weather and not for play, I'm going with … you're 'It'." She tagged him quickly and told Ginnie to run.

"That's not fair!" Uncle Jake whined, doing a pretty good imitation of a pouty kid.

"I learned from the best." Miss Amanda positioned his hands like a ballerina and went after her next victim. It didn't take long to catch Pete Jr., who was too busy laughing at Uncle Jake to move from Miss Amanda.

She planted one of his hands on his hip and the other pointing toward Uncle Jake, in a scolding fashion.

"He looks a little like you, dear," Austin's dad teased his mom. He backed up, but got pushed forward by Austin's mom, Miss Lauren.

Miss Amanda froze him to look like a gorilla.

Ginnie laughed hard, but kept her distance. Miss Amanda seemed determined to catch everyone quickly. She caught Austin when he tried to free his dad. Toran freed Austin, but got caught when he tried to free Uncle Jake.

Dad came around the corner at the same time Miss Amanda shooed Miss Lauren away from Uncle Jake. Apparently she didn't want Uncle Jake running around free. She invited Dad, Pierce, and Tillie to play along.

"How do you play?" Pierce asked.

Miss Amanda pointed at Uncle Jake. "It's a game of tag where you have to stand still in whatever position the person who's 'It' puts you. Someone else can tag you 'alive'. Then you try to tag the 'It' person and turn them into a statue. The 'It' person tries to tag everybody before they get tagged. But only someone who's been a statue can make the 'It' person a statue. We keep going until I make everyone a statue or they make *me* one."

Pierce grinned. "Sounds like fun." He ran out of Miss Amanda's reach, but Dad didn't.

She posed him as a "thinker" rubbing his chin.

Austin freed Uncle Jake and he tagged Miss Amanda.

Once Uncle Jake was 'It' the game was really on. He could outrun everyone but Dad.

Austin got posed as a baby sucking his thumb. Toran was fashioned into a moose with hand antlers. Pierce was positioned into Superman about to fly. Uncle Jake posed Dad and Miss Amanda in a kissing pose and for once, Dad didn't protest Uncle Jake's sneaky tactics.

Ginnie and Uncle Jake did a sort of dance around the kissing couple, keeping them in the middle. Ginnie finally bolted behind Austin's dad and Uncle Jake froze him as a fisherman casting a line.

Tillie unfroze Pierce, and got frozen into a ballerina for her efforts. Mrs. Owens tried to free Toran and got molded into a teapot. When Pierce stopped and laughed, Uncle Jake froze him into a saluting soldier. Pete Jr. freed the kissing couple, but they didn't want to move, so Uncle Jake froze them again, this time wrapping Dad's arms around Miss Amanda.

Again, Dad didn't seem to mind.

Ginnie took a long look at them, catching a glimmer in Dad's eyes and a matching one in Miss Amanda's.

A happy feeling washed over her ... just in time for Uncle Jake to ruin it by freezing her into a frog.

CHAPTER SIXTY:
SUNDAY

Ginnie woke the next morning when Dad opened her satin emerald curtains to let in the sun.

Remembering yesterday's visit, she sat up. "Do you think Pierce and his mom can come over today? We had fun yesterday."

Dad smiled. "I don't know. Uncle Ben's going to take them to visit Ray after church. I suspect he'll invite them over for lunch. You know how Uncle Ben is."

Ginnie returned Dad's smile. "I like how he is."

"Yeah? Me too." Dad jiggled her foot. "Come on, we have chores to do."

"Coming." Ginnie hopped out of bed.

Dad crossed her room to go into Toran's.

It didn't take long to finish her chores and dress for church. Since Dad was dating Miss Amanda now, they made room for her and Tillie in their pew. Dad only had to give them "the look" once before Tillie made sure he didn't catch them chatting again.

Tillie wasn't as much fun now that their folks were dating, at least not when Dad was around. "You know, he doesn't expect us to be perfect," Ginnie whispered.

"I know, but no sense in making him mad either."

Ginnie wondered briefly if Tillie was afraid of Dad or if she just wanted to impress him. She made a mental note to ask later, when her friend wouldn't shush her for talking in church.

During Sunday school, Ginnie could hardly contain her frustration when the teacher talked about forgiving people who hurt you. She didn't have a problem with forgiving her dad for making her paint the fence when he thought she was just being impulsive.

Or for forgiving Toran when he was being dumb about thinking she shouldn't stick up for him. Or for forgiving Pierce, when he twisted her wrist—especially since things turned out so awful for him.

But she *did* have a problem with Pierce having to forgive Mr. Owens for hurting him, or thinking Tillie should have to forgive Mr. Taylor for being mean to her and Miss Amanda. *That's just wrong.*

On the way home from church, she rode with Miss Amanda and Tillie. Whenever she thought about Pierce's bruised face and the lesson on forgiveness, she got mad all over again.

After Miss Amanda pulled into a parking spot, she got out and called Tillie over to her. "Tils, please go see what you can do to help Vi."

"Sure, Mom."

Ginnie started to follow her friend. Miss Amanda reached a hand to stop her. "Can I see you for a minute?"

Since "no" wasn't really an option, Ginnie stopped and searched Miss Amanda's face. She seemed concerned about something. "Am I in trouble?"

"Of course not."

Hmmm. *That's different.*

"Honest, you're not in trouble. Should you be?"

Ginnie shrugged. "*I* don't think so. But sometimes I am, even when I don't think I should be."

Miss Amanda smiled and drew her into a hug. "I was just wondering why you were angry."

"I'm not."

"You were looking pretty mad."

"I'm not though."

"Well that's good ... if it's true." Miss Amanda leaned toward her. "But I don't believe it."

Ginnie backed up. "I'm fine." As the words crossed her lips, her gaze dropped to the ground.

"You don't have to be afraid to talk to me," Miss Amanda whispered.

"I'm not." *Who could be afraid of Miss Amanda?*

"Well, if you're not mad *and* you're not afraid of me, why won't you talk to me?"

Lifting her head, Ginnie wondered the same thing. She shrugged and looked away, not being able to meet Miss Amanda's kind eyes.

"Did I do something wrong?" she asked.

Ginnie giggled a lame giggle. "You *never* do anything wrong. Neither does Tillie."

"Well ... then please tell me what's on your mind."

Sighing, Ginnie tried to put her crazy, mixed up feelings into words. "You shouldn't have to forgive Mr. Taylor for hurting you. And Tillie shouldn't either."

There ... it was out. *And* it didn't sound crazy.

Miss Amanda looked puzzled. "What brought that on?"

She thinks I'm nuts. Ginnie whirled from her.

Ginnie felt gentle hands on her shoulders. "Gin?"

"I'm not wrong." Ginnie crossed her arms.

"I didn't say you were. I'm trying to figure out *why* you're angry and why you're thinking about Jasper of all people."

Ginnie turned backed to her. "Because *he* was wrong. He shouldn't have hurt you and Tillie. And *he* should be saying he's sorry, *not you.*"

"Who said I should apologize to him?"

"My teacher."

"Mrs. Johnson?"

"No ... at church."

Miss Amanda shook her head, confused. "Why don't you start at the beginning and I'll see if I can catch up?"

Ginnie explained about the lesson on forgiveness and how she didn't mind forgiving the people who hurt *her* feelings, but didn't think Tillie, Miss Amanda, or Pierce should have to forgive the mean people in *their* lives.

Miss Amanda hugged her close. "Your dad's right. You are one loyal friend."

"You make it sound like a bad thing."

Miss Amanda looked behind her when they heard tires crunching down the dirt and gravel lane.

Daddy and Uncle Jake.

"Come on, let's go for a walk." Miss Amanda offered her hand and walked up the path toward the main barn. "It's definitely *not* a bad thing. I wish I had a friend like you when I was Tillie's age."

"Why?"

"Because you're brave. You're not afraid to say what's on your mind and you give the people around you courage. That's a pretty special gift you have."

"Dad calls it stubborn. *He* doesn't think it's so cool."

"Not true. He admires you. He told me."

"Really?" A fuzzy warm feeling cascaded over Ginnie.

"Yes. He's like me. Shy. *You* make him *have* to be brave, so he can keep up with you."

Ginnie let her words tumble around in her mind. *Hmmm.* "He doesn't *act* scared."

"I didn't say he was afraid. I *said* he was *shy*. There's a big difference. He's perfectly happy to go about his life taking care of his kids, going to work, working here on the farm. Doing the right things and not having drama." Miss Amanda slipped her arm around Ginnie's shoulder.

"Then you and Tillie decide you need to be 'for real' sisters and he has to decide if he's going to open his heart again after losing your mom. Of course *I* think he made the right decision to try again, but it was hard for him."

Ginnie rolled her eyes. "Because he's an ostrich."

Miss Amanda laughed. "Exactly."

"Well, *that's* a no-brainer. You're nice, Tillie's nice. Why shouldn't he date you?"

"Because something could happen to me. And that would hurt him … again."

Ginnie rolled her eyes again. "Why worry about that? You're just fine and so is he. That's dumb."

Miss Amanda smiled. "Because when you're shy and you've been hurt, you *do* worry about getting hurt again."

"That seems like a waste of time … to worry about something that probably won't happen."

"You are one smart girl, Ginnie West. You are *absolutely* right." Miss Amanda stopped walking and pulled Ginnie to her until their foreheads touched. "And *that's* why I forgave Jasper for hurting me."

Ginnie shook her head. "*That* doesn't make sense."

"If I hold a grudge, what is my heart full of?"

"Anger?"

"Exactly … and fear and hate. It's hard to *feel* love and kindness at the same time you feel fear and hate."

After considering her words, Ginnie shook her head again. "I don't get it. If you forgive him, doesn't he win?"

"Win what? *I* have Tillie. I'm happy. Jasper has nothing." Miss Amanda brushed Ginnie's bangs out of her face. "Forgiving isn't about letting someone get away with being mean. It's about feeling peace when you've been hurt. It took me a long time to learn that. But it's true."

Hmmm. Ginnie wanted to believe Miss Amanda but it still didn't quite make sense. She looked toward the farmhouse. Dad stood watching them. He smiled when Ginnie met his gaze. "Okay. If you say so."

"I do say so." Miss Amanda hugged her tight. "Being afraid feels lousy. And besides, to hold a grudge, I'd have to think about Jasper and I'd much rather think about you, your dad, Toran, and Tillie."

Ginnie giggled and hugged her back. "Okay, now *that* part makes sense."

CHAPTER SIXTY-ONE:
THE VISIT

Pierce squelched the urge to flee, his knees wobbling like gelatin. In the Sunday morning sun he eyed the bleak gray cinder block building where he would visit his father via videophone linkup.

His stomach lurched at the thought of soon being face-to-face with his father. Pierce swallowed hard, his eyes darting between Mom and Uncle Ben.

Mom's hand trembled, ever so slightly.

Uncle Ben wore an encouraging smile.

The longer he watched Uncle Ben, the calmer Pierce felt ... as if Uncle Ben were sharing his gentle strength.

I can do this.

Uncle Ben placed a hand on his shoulder. "It'll be fine. He's in another building. Say what you want. He'll have time to think about it before you see him again in person. He owes you a bit of understanding and he knows that."

"I want him to come home ... if he's sorry." Pierce chewed his thumb nail. "But I don't, if he's not."

"I understand." Uncle Ben looked him in the eye. "He knows he handled things wrong and only has himself to blame for being in jail."

Mom blinked away tears. "Dad loves us. Uncle Ben said if we don't feel safe with him, we have a place to go. It'll be okay." She paused, wiping her palms on her black slacks. "Being arrested has helped Dad realize he was out of control. Jail is like time out for adults. I want to believe he'll change. If he does, we'll support him. If he doesn't, we *will* leave. Your safety is my only concern."

Pierce steeled his gaze on her. "Do you mean it?"

Mom hugged him. "Of course. I remember a lesson Uncle Ben taught my Sunday school class years ago. He said 'doing the right thing isn't always easy, but it is always worth it.' If I'd remembered that when Dad started being mean—we wouldn't be here today."

Uncle Ben glanced at his watch. "The visit starts soon. Pierce, your dad can apologize to you and you can decide if he's sincere or not. I'm here for you. Are you ready?"

Pierce took in a sharp breath and held it a few seconds before blowing it out. Nodding, he rubbed his sweaty palms on his jeans.

Uncle Ben smiled, held the door open, and waited for them to walk through. Uncle Ben and Mom showed their driver's licenses and were directed to the next room.

Thirty phones lined the walls in the light blue room. A plastic chair sat in front of most of them. Pierce followed them to a booth with a number four stenciled on it.

Uncle Ben scooted three chairs together. "Marsha, would you like to sit in the middle?"

Mom nodded and sat.

Uncle Ben motioned to the two remaining chairs.

"This is kinda cool." Pierce sat and stared at the blue screen that said: "visit pending."

Uncle Ben laughed. "Yes. Very sci-fi. This technology was only dreamed of when I was a kid."

Mom sighed. "I wish it was under better circumstances."

"Hey look." Pierce pointed at the screen. "There he is."

Dad sat in an orange jumpsuit darting his eyes around the room. *He looks nervous. Good.*

Uncle Ben handed the phone to Mom. "Hi, Ray."

Pierce leaned closer to her and heard his father's voice. "Hi, Marsh. Can Pierce hear me?"

Pierce gave half a nod.

Dad seemed relieved. "Hi, Pierce. How are you?"

Mom tilted the phone toward him.

"Fine. And you?"

"Good as can be expected. Sorry you have to see me like this. I told Ben not to bring you, but I see he didn't listen." Dad shot a glare at Uncle Ben. "But I'll be home soon. They can't keep me here much longer. I need a real shower and some decent food." Familiar swear words crossed Dad's lips.

Chills ran down Pierce's spine. *Where's the apology? Dad just seems sorry for himself.* Pierce sent a questioning look to Uncle Ben.

Uncle Ben shook his head at the monitor and spoke in a stern voice. "Ray, we talked about this. Swearing doesn't show respect or that you want to make amends. Your family deserves better."

An old fear jumped into Pierce's throat when Dad grimaced. Uncle Ben and Dad exchanged cross looks and Pierce fought an urge to smile. *Wow, Uncle Ben's just calling him out. I'm so glad Dad can't reach us. He even looks a little scared. Good. It's his turn.*

"Ray, I won't be treated like that anymore. I'm here because I was told you want to fix things." Mom's confident tone surprised Pierce. "You can start by apologizing and meaning it."

Dad's scowl disappeared as his jaw dropped open. It had been a long time since Mom stood up to him in any meaningful way.

A warm feeling washed over Pierce. *Good going, Mom.* Pierce couldn't hear what Dad said, but he looked a little like a kicked puppy.

Mom handed him the phone. "He wants to talk to you, Pierce."

"Hi, Dad. Don't be mad, okay?" The reality of talking to him squashed any amusement at his father's discomfort. Being in jail a few more days wouldn't change him much.

"I'm not, Pierce. Well, not at you. I shouldn't have hurt you and I'm angry with myself that I did. You're a great kid and your mom's right; you both deserve to be treated better. If you'll be there when I get home, I'll prove it to you. Okay?" Dad's words seemed too syrupy.

"Sure, Dad. I'd like that."

"Maybe we can go to the movies or I'll buy you a new video game. You'd like that, wouldn't you?" Dad's smile grew wider. "We can get some pizza and ice cream. And a new DVD, okay?"

Pierce nodded as a sick feeling crept over him. *Dad's not sorry. He just wants to bribe me.*

"What's wrong?" An irritated edge stained Dad's tone. "We can do something else."

"Nothing's wrong, that sounds great. We'll have fun together." The words crossed his lips like sandpaper. "Hey, Uncle Ben gave me a baby hog. Maybe you can come see him. His name's Hamilton."

Dad's eyes flared as he hissed. "He's not your uncle. Can't you see he's trying to drive a wedge between us? You and me ... we can start over. You'll act better and I won't get so mad. *Okay?!*"

Pierce nodded automatically, fear and fury percolating in his belly. He glanced at Mom.

"Did he apologize?" Mom mouthed.

Pierce shrugged and put his hand over the receiver. "A little."

Mom took the phone. "So Ray, what do we do now?"

Pierce tuned out the rest of the conversation, concentrating on the tiny version of his father in the monitor. He sat in a cubicle built of gray cinder blocks in an orange jump suit. His hair was greasy. His unshaven chin was scruffy. The bland background made him seem small and more approachable.

I still want to know if he's sorry he hurt me or just sorry he got caught. Pierce focused on his dad for a clue.

"I mean it Ray. I'll give you another chance, but *only* one. I love you and so does Pierce." Mom's voice had a sad, reserved quality to it.

Pierce leaned closer to Mom so he could hear his father. "Marsha, let me talk to him again, please."

Please? Dad never says please. Pierce took the phone. "Pierce, I love you, do you know that?"

Pierce nodded, not trusting his own feelings or Dad's words, even though he wanted too.

"I can't hear your head rattle," Dad snapped, seeming to jump through the monitor. "I asked you a question. Do you know I love you?"

"S-sure, Dad. I know. I love you too. But ......"

"But what?" Dad tilted his head, his tone irritated.

"A-a-are you sorry you hurt me?"

Dad pasted a frustrated snarl on his face. "I already said I was, didn't you listen?"

Pierce's fear and fury jumped from his belly to his throat. He looked at Uncle Ben. Pierce put the phone against his chest. "He just said that he *said* he was sorry, but he didn't. Now he's mad."

"Tell him what you want to, Pierce. He might be angry now, but he's not going anywhere for a few more days. And remember, you can have a counselor present to get used to each other before he comes back home. And I'll talk with him again as well."

"Are you sure?"

Uncle Ben nodded. "Yes, I'm sure."

"Okay." Pierce startled as he lifted the receiver and heard Dad yelling to talk to him. "Dad, I'm here."

Dad scowled into the monitor. "What's he saying?"

Pierce's eyes flicked from the monitor to Uncle Ben. He wiped his hand on his jeans. "He says I should tell you what I really think."

Dad sputtered a protest and then stopped. "Well, okay, as long as he isn't telling you to hate me."

"He wouldn't do that. He wants our family to get back together. But he doesn't want Mom and me to be scared anymore."

The tension eased from Dad's face some. "Okay. That's good to know. I love you."

"I know you do, Dad. I love you, too." Pierce glanced at the screen. "But I want to know if you're *really* sorry. You didn't *say* you were sorry for hurting me. Just that you were mad at yourself for hurting me. I want to know you're really sorry and won't hurt me again."

Dad's scowl returned and his jaw clamped together. "I said—" His voice trailed off as his eyes darted to each of them. He hesitated and licked his lips. His eyes seemed to bore into Pierce. "I'm sorry. I really am. You didn't deserve to be knocked down or kicked. I'm not good at apologies or feelings, but I'll try harder, okay?"

Pierce nodded. "Okay. I just wanted to hear you're sorry and mean it. I want you to come home. But I don't want to be afraid of you. When you're not mad, I like to be around you."

A pained look crossed Dad's face. "I don't want you to be afraid of me. I hated it when my mom made me feel that way. Sorry."

The bumble bees left. "Sure, Dad. Everyone deserves a second chance." For the first time in a long time, a warm smile lighted on Dad's lips. "Thanks, Pierce. I promise I'll be a better dad to you. I didn't have a dad, but I'll figure it out. You can help me, okay?"

"Sure."

"I love you, Pierce. I owe your mom an apology too. Can you

give her the phone?"

"Yes." Pierce grinned and handed Mom the phone. "He apologized and I think he meant it, *this* time."

Mom took the phone and smiled.

Pierce sat back. *I'm glad I told him the truth. Maybe Dad can change.* He peeked at the monitor.

Dad had a smug look on his face.

The bumblebees returned.

Uncle Ben invited Pierce and his mom back to the farm after they saw his father. Pierce hurried to the side porch when he found out it was time to feed the piglet again. "Can I keep coming out to feed Hamilton?"

"Sure. And if it's okay with your mom, you can train him and raise him for fair next year. Would you like that?" Uncle Ben asked.

"Yes! Mom, can I?"

Mom shook her head. "I-I don't know. He's little now, but we couldn't keep him at the house when he gets bigger."

"Marsha, you can certainly keep him at your house for the next couple weeks until he's as big as his brothers and sisters if you want. But I meant that Pierce was welcome to come out here as often as he can and work with Hamilton. Pigs make good pets, but Hamilton would be happier here."

"Could we do that?" Excitement pulsed through Pierce. He grabbed his mom's arm. "We could keep him at home until Dad gets back, and then come to the farm after that?"

Mom laughed, relieved. "*That* we can do. I don't think your dad would do well with a pig in the house."

Good, then we can keep coming to the farm. Pierce still didn't like Ginnie much, but her family was kinda cool. They didn't yell and Toran had quite a collection of animals. The babies were his favorite. Maybe if Dad got some help, he might even say yes to a new kitten. Pierce had his eye on the biggest gray one.

CHAPTER SIXTY-TWO:
PART ONE OF THE PLAN

The contrast between the angry, defensive Pierce who came out to the farm with his dad a few days ago and the bruised, but kinder, "regular-kid" Pierce who visited over the weekend, had Ginnie puzzling the rest of Sunday to find a way to make school on Monday easier for Pierce.

Toran, Austin, Tillie, and Ginnie talked amongst each other to form a plan.

When Monday morning arrived, they were ready.

Dad drove the four of them to school a little early.

Ginnie and Tillie hurried to find Mrs. Johnson before the rest of the students arrived.

"Good morning, girls. You're here early today," Mrs. Johnson greeted pleasantly.

"Good morning," they chorused, with Ginnie rushing on to add. "We need to talk. It's important."

Mrs. Johnson walked over to the door, looked around the hallway, and then closed the door. "All right. I have a few minutes. What do we need to talk about?"

"Pierce," Tillie blurted.

Mrs. Johnson took in a quick breath. "Did you get into another fight with him?"

"No. His dad beat him up and got arrested," Ginnie added and shook her head. "He's our friend now."

She thought about Pierce being more open with Toran than

herself and continued. "Well, *mostly* our friend. We're *his* friend more than he's *our* friend, but that's okay."

The teacher's hands flew to her mouth as her eyes popped open wide. "Is he okay?"

Tillie shook her head.

Ginnie shrugged. "His face looks even more horrible, but he'll be okay."

"What happened?"

Tillie and Ginnie took turns filling her in on the events of the weekend and finished with, "I thought about what you said. Can you help *us* help *him*? We have some ideas."

"Of course. Let me know what's on your mind," Mrs. Johnson said.

Tillie and Ginnie exchanged smiles. They tumbled over each other's words, telling her their plan.

CHAPTER SIXTY-THREE: THE WAITING GAME

Toran and Austin paced the whole length of Mr. Reed's waiting room while Dad sat in a chair along the wall.

"What's taking them so long?" Toran asked.

Dad folded and unfolded a magazine he held in his hand, but didn't read. "They have a lot to talk about. Try to be patient."

Toran didn't want to be patient. He wanted the principal to release Pierce. He wanted to act on the plan 'The Four Musketeers' came up with yesterday.

A sudden influx of students swarmed through the two sets of front double doors. Toran scanned the mass of bodies for Levi and Steve.

Finally, he spotted them. Levi escorted Steve to the principal's office like they had planned.

Dad stood. "Hi, Levi." He arched a questioning eyebrow at Toran after spotting Steve.

Toran made the introduction. "Dad, this is Steve."

Dad extended his hand. "It's nice to meet you Steve. I hear you're a friend of Pierce's."

Steve nodded suspiciously and shook his hand. "Yeah."

"Good. Pierce can use a lot of good friends right now. He's speaking with Mr. Reed. He'll be out in a moment."

Toran eyed Steve. "Did Levi tell you what happened?"

"Yeah. That happens a lot. But his dad's never been arrested before," Steve said.

A wave of fury and nausea rolled over Toran. "You knew?"

Steve shrugged. "What am I supposed to do about it? Pierce didn't want anyone else to know. And I'm not messing with his old man. He's a mean dude."

Dad reached a firm hand to Toran's shoulder just as Toran opened his mouth. "Toran, why don't you fill Steve in on your plan to help Pierce today?"

Toran swallowed his anger and tried to focus his thoughts on the mission at hand. "Okay." He motioned Dad, Steve, and Levi into a corner when two students came through the door.

He lowered his voice. "I only have two classes with Pierce, but you guys are with him all day, on and off. Pierce doesn't want everyone knowing his business, and I don't blame him."

Levi nodded his agreement. "Me either."

"If his face is as bruised as you say it is, people are gonna know," Steve pointed out.

"Well, *we* don't have to talk about it. If Pierce wants people to know, *he* can tell them," Toran insisted. "And if *he* doesn't want to talk about it, we can change the subject or run interference for him. Like just remind him we have to get to class."

"Or tell people to quit staring, or not make a big deal about how he looks, so other kids don't," Austin added.

"And sit with him at lunch. Just don't act pathetic or like you feel sorry for him. He'll hate that," Levi said.

Each nodded and murmured.

"Most people aren't going to mess with him, they don't usually," Steve reminded them.

"Those aren't the people I'm worried about. It's the ones who'll point and stare." Toran stood straighter, wanting to pound the non-existent offenders at the thought. "Or worse, crack bad jokes and make fun of him."

"I'll take care of *them*," Steve threatened.

Dad cleared his throat.

Toran shook his head. "As tempting as that is, violence is how we got here. *More* violence isn't gonna help."

Steve rolled his eyes. "Yeah, I forgot, you let your sister do your fighting for you. I thought you wanted to be Pierce's friend now?"

Bristling, Toran clenched and unclenched his fists.

Dad gave an almost imperceptible shake of his head.

Toran remembered something Dad often said to him and Ginnie. "Steve, you can be part of the problem or part of the solution. You don't have to be *my* friend, but you could at least try to be *his*."

"I *am* his friend." Steve's nostrils flared. His eyes narrowed angrily, before his expression softened. "Where's your sister?"

"Working on another part of our plan with Tillie." Austin smiled at Steve. "She's Pierce's friend now *too*, so you probably don't want to mess with her. You saw what she did to *Pierce,* when he went after Toran."

Toran cringed at Austin's words, but almost smiled when a look of horror crossed Steve's face.

Steve recovered quickly and toggled his head. "Well, I was Pierce's friend *first,* so she better not mess with *me*."

Dad coughed into his fist.

Steve's self-confident smirk dimmed.

"We're all on the same side now. You don't have anything to worry about." Toran glanced at Dad, who gave a quick nod. "We're here to help Pierce, *together*. We can *all* be part of the solution. Mr. Reed's on board with us, so anybody being a problem gets to deal with *him*."

He tried not to look too happy when a green hue washed over Steve. They both knew Steve was no stranger to Mr. Reed's office. "Okay then, we're ready when Pierce is."

As if on cue, Mr. Reed's door opened.

CHAPTER SIXTY-FOUR:
FRIENDS

S o Pierce, I just want you to know that we will do whatever we can to help you through this difficult time. I'm calling an assembly today for all the sixth graders ... just to remind kids about the golden rule: treating others the way they want to be treated."

Panic seized Pierce. "Everybody's gonna know it's about me. They'll stare and worse."

Mr. Reed offered an encouraging smile. "You and your friends don't have to attend. Something more fun has been planned for you instead."

"Really?" Pierce glanced suspiciously at the principal. "What friends? I mean *which* friends?"

"Let's go see." Mr. Reed motioned at the door.

Feeling relief at Mr. Reed's assurance that he would do whatever he could to help to make Pierce's day go better, Pierce shook the principal's offered hand and smiled.

Mom also shook Mr. Reed's hand. They followed the principal into the waiting room.

Pierce nearly walked into Mom, stunned to see Steve, Levi, Austin, Toran, and Toran's dad waiting for them. His first reaction was to hide behind Mom, but then he remembered that Toran and Austin had already seen his face and they didn't act like it mattered.

Toran's dad smiled at him, reminding him a little of Uncle Ben, whom he had grown to really like over the weekend.

Steve walked over to him. "So dude, we got your back. Anybody messes with *you*, messes with *us*."

Pierce liked the sentiment of Steve's words.

"What he *means*—" Toran said, stepping quickly next to Steve. "Is we want to show you that you have a bunch of friends now. We won't blab your business and we'll be with you all day." He pointed between the boys. "Well, we'll be taking turns walking with you, since we don't all have the same classes. In a couple days, people will be used to you being our friend. You can make new ones too."

Toran's words weren't as direct as Steve's, but they had a nice feel to them.

"Well, I can look out for myself." Pierce scanned the room again quickly, assessing each kid. "But I'll let you hang out with me."

The last thing he needed was people feeling sorry for him. But it wouldn't hurt to have some kids he hoped he could trust around. This weekend had felt nice, even if he did have to spend it with Ginnie. Toran and Austin had turned out to be pretty cool.

"Epic." Austin offered him a fist to bump. "My brother says if you want to come out to our place to ride horses, he'll let me ride Ranger so you can ride Traxx."

Riding horses again appealed to him, even though his legs were a little sore from last time.

"I have to go take care of Hamilton anyway. We could ride the horses as well, huh Mom?" Pierce answered.

"If that's okay with the Chandler's, I'm fine with it."

A nice feeling came over him, like warm syrup over pancakes.

He fist-bumped with Austin again. "Epic."

CHAPTER SIXTY-FIVE:
PART TWO OF THE PLAN

During second period, all of the six graders were called into an assembly in the gymnasium, except Pierce, Steve, Ginnie, Tillie, Austin, Levi, Tuck, and Toran. The seven of them met in Mrs. Johnson's room and put the next part of "The Four Musketeer's" plan in motion.

"Ginnie, why don't you let everyone know why we are here?" Mrs. Johnson said.

"Sure." Ginnie stood. "As you all know, the last day of school is Thursday and we're having a carnival the last two periods of the day to celebrate. We need to make and man a couple of booths. So Mrs. Johnson said we can plan them this period and work on them during lunch for the next couple of days."

"Cool. So what are the booths?" Tuck asked.

"We have to think of some," Tillie said.

"My mom has a lollipop tree holder," Austin volunteered. "We fill it with lollipops after we color the bottoms of the sticks in random colors. The colors match up to prizes in different buckets. Like the duck pond game without water."

"Candy and a prize?" Steve licked his lips. "That's a good deal. But we need to make the other booth more complicated."

"Like what?" Pierce asked, and then slapped his leg, apparently inspired. "What about a dunking booth? We could dunk the principal. People would pay a lot of money for *that*."

Everyone laughed.

"Yeah … and I'd pay to dunk Mr. Hammond. I hate history," Steve said.

"Where are you going to get a dunk tank?" Mrs. Johnson asked.

"We could build one," Austin suggested.

Toran shook his head. "By Thursday?"

Austin shrugged. "Hey, it's a good idea. We should try to make it work."

Pierce beamed.

"It's a good idea, but we don't have time to build it." Tillie tapped her chin. "But I think we should do something fun like that."

"How about shooting cans with our air soft guns? We do it all the time out at the farm," Toran suggested.

"You do?" Pierce asked, turning to him. "That sounds like fun. Can we do that when I come out to feed Hamilton sometime?"

"Sure." Toran's grin widened. "Uncle Jake just gave us a whole bunch of ammunition for our birthday."

"Slow down guys," Mrs. Johnson cautioned. "As fun as that sounds, there is a school policy against guns on the premises, even air-soft rifles. I don't think we can do that."

"Aw man. We weren't gonna shoot them at *people*," Pierce complained.

"I know, but it's still school policy," Mrs. Johnson said.

Tuck shrugged. "Maybe we can rent a dunk tank? That's still a good idea."

"Where do we rent it from?" Austin paced a few feet. "And won't that cost a lot?"

"I dunno. I just like the idea of a dunk tank," Tuck insisted.

"What about a roping contest?" Ginnie suggested. "We could set up a practice saddle with attached horns on a bale of hay and people can rope a pretend steer? It's harder than it looks and different than what other people will come up with."

Tillie smiled. "That would be cool."

Toran nodded. "We have all the stuff. It wouldn't cost anything."

"But where's the challenge if it doesn't move? Could we rope a *real* calf?" Pierce swept a finger from Toran to Ginnie. "That would be fun. You guys have a herd of cows."

"We'd have to get a huge pen." Toran shook his head. "And it wouldn't be much fun for the calves to get roped over and over. We couldn't bring many to school."

"And someone would have to clean up after them. Do you want *that* job?" Ginnie laughed when Pierce's face scrunched into a grimace.

"How hard can it be to rope a saddle that doesn't move?" Steve asked.

"Harder than you think. Especially if you have to get it around the horns." Ginnie snapped her fingers. "*That* would be part of the attraction. People would think it's easy and since it's really not, they would keep trying to beat it. We could make a lot of money."

"Good idea," Austin added. "And it's fun. Can we Mrs. Johnson?"

Their teacher nodded. "I don't see why not. I've seen a lot of carnival games over the years here, but that's one game we've never done here before."

"Then it's settled. This'll be the coolest carnival ever," Pierce declared.

CHAPTER SIXTY-SIX:
LETTERS

When the dismissal bell rang, Ginnie and Tillie stayed in Mrs. Johnson's class because they had her for English next.

The boys made their way to their own classes.

Ginnie was sorry to see them go.

"That was fun," Tillie said, snapping Ginnie back to reality.

"It was. I think we'll have the best game at the carnival."

"I'm really happy to see you take charge like this, girls. Pierce needs some friends and something positive to focus on." Mrs. Johnson handed them each a certificate she reserved for when one of her students got caught going the extra mile for someone else.

Ginnie glanced at hers. It was for a free homework pass. "Cool, but you don't have to reward me for doing the right thing. I like Pierce now, even if he doesn't completely like me." She handed back the pass.

Mrs. Johnson held up her hand in a 'stop' motion. "You might need that this week. You're going to be busy working on your carnival game." She smiled at each of them. "Besides, moments like these really make my day and remind me why I became a teacher in the first place. It's nice to see my students making a positive difference in each other's lives."

Ginnie and Tillie traded happy grins.

Their classmates started pouring through the door.

"Please take your seats, everyone. Class is about to start." Mrs. Johnson clapped her hands to quiet the growing din of voices. "We have a special assignment to go along with today's assembly."

Ginnie and Tillie made their way to their desks.

"I want you to think about your best friend and consider what qualities they have that make them a good friend. Then write your friend a letter sharing your thoughts." Mrs. Johnson walked up one row of desks and down another. "Take your time. Write a letter that you would want to read twenty years from now. I recently ran across a letter like this from my best friend in fifth grade. It felt just as nice to read it now as it did when she wrote it."

Tillie raised her hand. "Can we write a letter to our best friend and to a *new* friend?"

"Of course. That's a wonderful idea." Mrs. Johnson walked to the front of the room and leaned against her desk. "Write a letter to your best friend, and if you have time, look around the room and see if you could write a letter to someone you don't normally hang out with, or someone you've passed in the hall that looked sad recently, or someone you want to get to know, but haven't. Or just write a quick thank you note to someone who has done something nice for you."

Ginnie exchanged smiles with Tillie and knew Pierce would be getting at least two letters today.

CHAPTER SIXTY-SEVEN: WE END AT THE BEGINNING

G innie and Tillie hurried to the cafeteria, each with a folded letter in their back pocket and a lunch sack in hand.

They reached their usual table shortly after Toran, Steve, Pierce, Austin, Levi, Maddy, Tuck, and Luci Jo did.

It was strange in a nice sort of way to have Pierce sitting with them. Ginnie thought about the things she wrote in her letter to Pierce. She hoped he would take them how she meant them, and not be weirded out.

Pierce stopped laughing when he saw her. He stared at her for a few seconds, and then turned his attention back to Toran and Steve.

The lead ball feeling she had when she was at his house the night his dad was arrested returned to her belly.

Well, at least Pierce likes THEM.

Now that she was with the rest of her friends, she felt strange giving Pierce the letter. Maybe later, when he came out to the farm would be better.

She sat across from Pierce, next to Tillie, in the only space left. Tillie glanced around the table and looked like she was having second thoughts as well. Tillie sat down and opened her sack, pulling out a sandwich, carrot sticks, ranch dip, and a drink.

Ginnie's own lunch had a ham sandwich, Cheetos and chocolate chip cookies that Vi made last night. Vi had packed extra cookies to share.

Good. Maybe that will break the ice with Pierce.

"Pierce, what happened to your face?"

Ginnie looked up. A boy named Devon that she didn't know very well stood next to Pierce.

Pierce stiffened.

She could tell that he had forgotten about his face and didn't want to be reminded. She didn't blame him. It looked better than yesterday, but was still multi-colored.

The lead ball dropped heavily as the kid smirked.

Pierce stood, straightening his shoulders menacingly. "What's it to you?"

Ginnie jumped to her feet, swallowing hard, feeling reminiscent of this exact staging a week ago.

The rest of her friends at the table rose as one.

Devon scanned the faces and shrugged. "Just wondering. No biggie."

Pierce glanced around the table. His defensive scowl turned to a line, then a small smile. He let his gaze rest on Ginnie's for a second. At first they seemed to hold a warning.

Then they softened along with the rest of his features.

Ginnie didn't expect that they would be best friends anytime soon, but Pierce seemed to realize that she meant well. And even if he didn't, she'd eventually get him to understand.

After all, Dad was right.

Wests don't do friendship halfway.

A MESSAGE FROM
THE AUTHOR:

If you want personalized signed copies of any of my books, please visit my website:

http://moniquebucheger.blogspot.com/

Please be my Facebook friend:

http://www.facebook.com/monique.bucheger

If you like my books, I would really appreciate it if you would leave a review at Amazon.com, Kobo.com, Goodreads.com, Barnesandnoble.com, and / or any other review site you use.

Type my name in the search bar: Monique Bucheger, and all of my books will show up. Please write a sentence or two about why you liked it. You can copy and paste the same review to each place. This would really help me reach new readers.

Thank you. ☺

-Monique Bucheger

ABOUT THE AUTHOR

MONIQUE BUCHEGER

When Monique isn't writing, you can find her playing taxi driver to one or more of her 12 children, plotting her next novel, scrapbooking, or being the "Mamarazzi" at any number of child-oriented events. Even though she realizes there will never be enough hours in any given day, Monique tries very hard to enjoy the journey that is her life. She shares it with a terrific husband, her dozen children, one adorable granddaughter, two cats, and many real and imaginary friends. She is the author of several books and hopes to write many more. You can find more about Monique and her works at:

www.moniquebucheger.blogspot.com

OTHER BOOKS BY MONIQUE BUCHEGER

The Secret Sisters Club: A Ginnie West Adventure

Simply West of Heaven: A Ginnie West Adventure

Being West is Best: A Ginnie West Adventure

The Ginnie West Adventure Collection Multi-Book set

(featuring Books 1-3)

Popcorn (A Picture Book featuring Ginnie and Toran when they were 3- before their mom died. Coming summer of 2014.)

For More Great Content
Including Free Downloads Visit:

www.moniquebucheger.blogspot.com

For more about about the illustrator, Mikey Brooks, visit:

www.insidemikeysworld.com

.

Made in USA - Kendallville, IN
1075315_9781939993106